KNIT
tops
for kids

Irresistible Projects
for Girls & Boys
Ages 1 to 6

Muriel Agator

STACKPOLE
BOOKS

To my children and my family, for their encouragement all the way through the development of this book.

To my nephew Gabin and my daughter Anuhea, models for a day . . .

To my precious knitting friends from the yarn-ball gang.

Thank you to Valérie and Isabelle and the whole Temps Apprivoisé team for sharing this adventure with me.

Thank you to Fifi Mandirac for her superb photo styling, and to Claire for the photos; you both knew so well how to immortalize all the joie de vivre of these bubbly little models, and I am grateful to each of you!

Thank you to my yarn partners: Barbara at Comptoir, Bergère de France, Cécile at Bouillon de couture, Gwendola at Laine et tricot, the triplets (Axelle, Peggy, and Rosalind) at Kaléidoscope, Sandra at L'échappée laine.

Thank you to Chloé from Bulles de gum for the lovely doll made for this occasion.

Thank you to the little models. In order of appearance: Anuhea, Léon, Esteban, Louisa, Manhaut, Gabin, Suzie, Charlie, Elisa.

And a very special thank you to my dear Laurence Mériat . . .

I would love to meet you on my blog, La Pelote Masquée (kidstricots.canalblog.com), and on my website, Kids Tricots (www.kids-tricots.fr).

Senior editor: Valérie Gendreau
Editor: Isabelle Riener
Proofreading: Annie Testart-Louange
Graphic design: Anne Bénoliel-Defréville
Cover design: Wendy A. Reynolds
Pagination: Coline de Graaf
Photography: Claire Curt
Photo styling: Fifi Mandirac
Production: Géraldine Boilley-Hautbois, Louise Martinez
Photoengraving: Nord Compo
Translation: Kathryn Fulton

© LIBELLA, Paris, 2012
This translation of *Irrésistibles À Tricoter 0 à 6 ans* first published in France by LIBELLA under the imprint LTA in 2012 is published by arrangement with Silke Bruenink Agency, Munich, Germany.
This edition © 2016 by Stackpole Books

Published by
STACKPOLE BOOKS
5067 Ritter Road
Mechanicsburg, PA 17055
www.stackpolebooks.com

Printed in the United States of America

10 9 8 7 6 5 4 3 2 1

First edition

Library of Congress Cataloging-in-Publication Data

Agator, Muriel, author.
  [Irrésistibles à tricoter. English]
  Knit tops for kids : irresistible projects for girls and boys ages 1 to 6 / Muriel Agator ; translation, Kathryn Fulton. — First edition.
       pages cm
  Translation of: Irrésistibles à tricoter : 0 à 6 ans, first published in France by LIBELLA under the imprint LTA in 2012.
  ISBN 978-0-8117-1664-2
  1. Knitting—Patterns. 2. Dressmaking—Patterns. 3. Children's clothing. I. Fulton, Kathryn, 1987– translator. II. Title.
  TT825.A38513 2016
  746.43'2—dc23
                                        2015030784

Preface

For as long as I can remember, I have always loved knitting. As soon as I learned how to knit, at the age of 9, I began creating designs for my dolls—then, at 13, for my first little niece, and later for my own children.

I have created some little knits for you that are easy to make and can be worn every day. Some are great for gifts or to knit while waiting for a baby's arrival. Bright colors or pastels: there's something here for all tastes! Some of the designs beg for you to add your own personal touch and embellishments.

I hope you will have as much fun knitting these designs as I had creating them.

Muriel Agator

Contents

Materials

❋ Yarn

Look for materials that are soft and easy to work with: alpaca (warm and light in winter, ideal for little ones), wool, cotton, as well as natural materials like rayon, which is absorbent and breathable at the same time. With a skein of yarn, start with the end of the yarn on the inside. For yarn sold in hanks, wind it into a ball before knitting; a yarn swift and a ball winder will help.

❋ Needles and Hooks

Use straight needles sizes 4 (3.5 mm), 6 (4 mm), 7 (4.5 mm), 8 (5 mm), 9 (5.5 mm), and 10 (6 mm) and crochet hooks sizes D-3 (3.25 mm), G-6 (4 mm), and H-8 (5 mm). You will also need circular needles in sizes 4 (3.5 mm), 6 (4 mm), 7 (4.5 mm), and 10 (6 mm) and a cable needle.

6

ABBREVIATIONS

We have used the following abbreviations in this book to write the instructions in a quick and easy-to-read format.

C6B	cable 6 back	**sc**	single crochet
C6F	cable 6 front	**skp**	slip, knit, pass slipped stitch over
ch	chain	**sk2p**	slip, knit 2 together, pass slipped stitch over
inc	increase (make 1)	**sl**	slip
k	knit	**sl st**	slip stitch
k2tog	knit 2 stitches together	**sm**	slip marker
p	purl	**st(s)**	stitch(es)
pm	place marker	**WS**	wrong side
pwise	purlwise	**wyif**	with yarn in front
RS	right side	**yo**	yarn over

❈ Circular Needles

Often associated with knitting in the round, these needles can also be used for knitting back and forth in rows like with straight needles. They can give you extra length thanks to the length of the cable, which can allow you to add a significant number of additional stitches; this is very useful for top-down designs (knit in a single piece, starting from the collar) or bottom-up designs (knit in a single piece, starting from the bottom), and pieces requiring a large number of stitches in a single row (such as for a back/front and sleeves). Avoid those with a cable that is very thick or rigid, which may make them difficult to work with.

There are several types of circular needles:

- fixed, with different lengths of cables—32 in./80 cm is sufficient for children's clothes; and 24 in./60 cm for baby clothes
- interchangeable, with cables that detach from the needles and allow you to customize the needle size and cable length to your needs

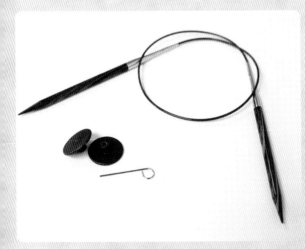

❈ Embellishments

Whimsical buttons, patches, or ribbons will add a personal touch to your projects.

❈ Stitch Markers

Ring-style stitch markers are indispensable; slide each marker onto the needle between two stitches and pass them from left to right needle as you knit. Use them to locate the right side, or to mark increases. Stitch markers come in many shapes, materials, and sizes. For the projects in this book, you will need 8 stitch markers.

❈ Stitch Holders

Stitch holders are used to keep stitches that are being set aside to work later. For the projects in this book, you will need 2.

Knitting Lesson

CASTING ON

Begin with a slip knot on the needle, leaving a long tail. Take the working yarn and place it in your left hand (for right-handed knitters). Pass the yarn across the palm and around the thumb (1). Hold the needle in your right hand, bring it through the loop on the left thumb, passing it under the strand of yarn (2), with the right hand, bring the tail yarn up and wrap it around the needle (3). Pull the yarn through the thumb loop, then drop the loop and tighten it to the needle: you have formed the first stitch. Repeat, wrapping the yarn around your left thumb, sliding the needle through the loop, then wrapping the tail yarn around the needle and pulling it back through: you have formed the second stitch. Repeat the process as many times as needed.

Be careful that your stitches don't become so tight that they will not slide easily along the needle!

KNIT (K)

The yarn is behind the work, which is on the left needle; work with the yarn wrapped over the right index finger.

1. Insert the right needle into the first stitch, under the left needle.
2. Wrap the yarn around the right needle, from bottom to top.
3. Bring the right needle gently down, bringing the point through the stitch, and bring it back to above the left needle.
4. Let the loop on the left needle drop: you have formed a new stitch on the right needle.
5. Repeat the process, stitch by stitch, so that all the stitches from the left needle pass to the right needle; you will obtain a new row of stitches.

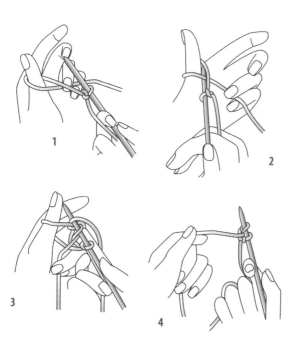

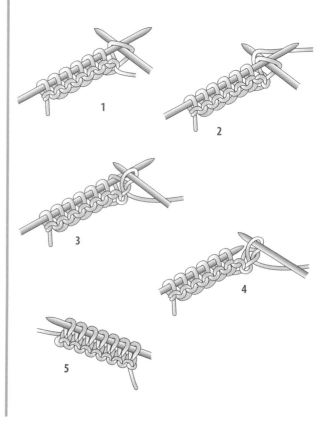

PURL (P)

The yarn is in front of the work.

1. Keeping the yarn in front of the right needle, insert the right needle into the first stitch on the left needle, with the right needle in front of the left needle.
2. Bring the yarn up and over the right needle.
3. Slide the right needle under the left needle.
4. Pull gently on the left needle to let the loop drop: you have formed a new stitch on the right needle.
5. Repeat the process, stitch by stitch, so that all the stitches from the left needle pass to the right needle; you will obtain a new row of stitches.

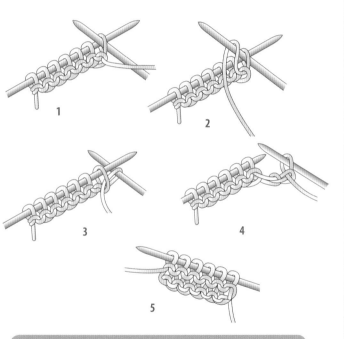

GAUGE

It's essential to check your gauge to avoid unpleasant surprises. If your gauge is off, a project may come out a very different size, your work may end up very loose (when it would have worked with a needle one size smaller), a collar may end up too tight, and so on, depending on how you knit. Only checking the gauge will ensure that your project comes out like the one in the pattern. If the gauge swatch you make is larger than the size indicated, use a needle one size down; if the gauge swatch is smaller, use a needle one size larger.

STOCKINETTE STITCH

Row 1 (RS): Knit all stitches.
Row 2: Purl all stitches.
Return to Row 1 and repeat these two rows throughout.
For stockinette stitch when working in the round, knit all stitches every round.

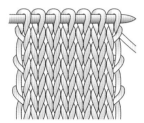

REVERSE STOCKINETTE STITCH

Row 1 (RS): Purl all stitches.
Row 2: Knit all stitches.
Return to Row 1 and repeat these two rows throughout.
For reverse stockinette stitch when working in the round, purl all stitches every round.

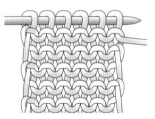

GARTER STITCH

Knit every row.
When working in the round, alternate one knit row with one purl row throughout.

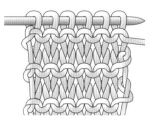

1X1 RIBBING

Row 1: Alternate 1 knit stitch and 1 purl stitch, being careful to place the yarn behind the work for the knit stitches and to bring it back to the front for the purl stitches.

For the following rows, work each stitch as it appears: knit the stitches that appear as knit in the previous row and purl those that look like purl stitches.

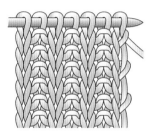

WHIMSICAL 2X1 RIBBING

Row 1: *K2, p1; repeat from * to end.
Row 2: Purl.

Return to Row 1 and repeat these two rows throughout.

WHIMSICAL 3X2 RIBBING

Row 1: *K3, p2; repeat from * to end.
Row 2: Purl.

Return to Row 1 and repeat these two rows throughout.

SEED STITCH

Row 1: Alternate k1, p1 (as for 1 x 1 ribbing, think about bringing the yarn to the correct side for the kind of stitch you're working).
Row 2: Knit the stitches that appear to be purl stitches in the previous row, and purl the stitches that look like knit stitches.

Return to Row 1 and repeat these two rows throughout.

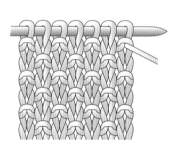

ALTERNATE SEED STITCH

Row 1: *K1, p1; repeat from * to end.
Row 2: Purl.

Return to Row 1 and repeat these two rows throughout.

SLIPPED STITCH (PURLWISE) (SL PWISE)

Bring the yarn to the front, insert the right needle into the next stitch on the left needle, then slide it to the right needle without knitting it.

KNIT 2 STITCHES TOGETHER (K2TOG)

Insert the right needle into the second stitch on the left needle (1), then catch the first stitch at the same time (2); next, bring the yarn around and knit through the two stitches at the same time, just as if you were only knitting one stitch (3).

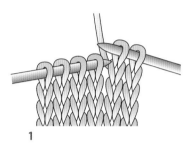

1

2

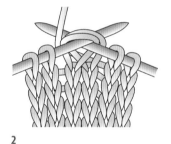

3

10

YARN OVER (YO)

This stitch is used to create open-work. Pass the working yarn over the right needle without knitting with it (1), then work the next stitch normally: you will have one additional stitch (2, 3). To keep the same number of stitches, you'll need to knit 2 together or work a slip, knit, pass.

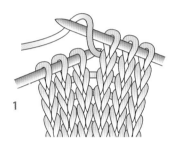

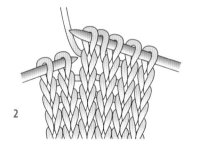

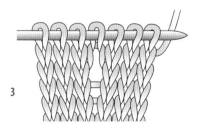

SLIP, KNIT, PASS (SKP)

Slip 1 stitch knitwise from the left needle to the right needle (1), knit the next stitch, then pass the slipped stitch over the knit stitch (2). You will have one fewer stitch (3).

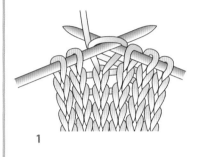

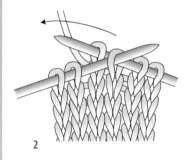

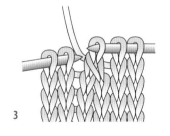

SLIP 1, KNIT 2 TOGETHER, PASS SLIPPED STITCH OVER (SK2P)

Slip 1 stitch knitwise onto the right needle (1), knit the next 2 stitches together (2), then pass the slipped stitch over the k2tog stitch (3). You will have two fewer stitches.

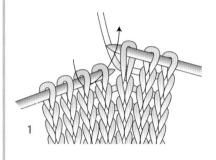

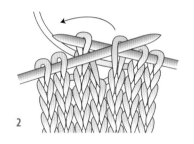

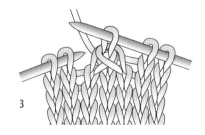

SIMPLE DECREASES 2 STITCHES FROM THE EDGE

At the beginning of a row, work 2 stitches normally, then decrease by knitting 2 stitches together (1); at the end of the row, when 4 stitches remain, work 1 skp, then work the last 2 stitches (2).

Variation: You can reverse the directions of the decreases to create raglan shaping with a different look: work the skp at the beginning of the row, and k2tog at the end of the row (see p. 18 for the Raglan Pullover).

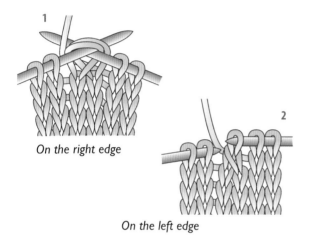

On the right edge

On the left edge

DOUBLE DECREASES 2 STITCHES FROM THE EDGE

At the beginning of a row, work 2 stitches normally, then decrease by knitting 3 stitches together; at the end of the row, when 5 stitches remain, work a sk2p, then work the last 2 stitches normally.

MAKE 1 INCREASES (INC)

To form the yoke of a raglan sweater, you'll need to work make 1 increases, paying attention to the direction of the stitch—first right-leaning, then left-leaning, for each group of increases.

- Make 1 right: With the right needle, pick up the strand of yarn between 2 stitches (1) and place it on the left needle, so that it goes from the front of the work to the back (2). Insert the right needle under this strand, twisting it (as indicated by the arrow in 2); wrap the yarn around the right needle and knit the stitch. You will obtain one new stitch that leans to the right.
- Make 1 left: With the right needle, pick up the strand of yarn in between 2 stitches and place it on the left needle, so that it goes from the back of the work to the front (1). Insert the right needle into this new loop, bringing it up under the back strand and behind the left needle (2). Wrap the yarn around the right needle and knit the stitch. You will obtain one new stitch that leans to the left.

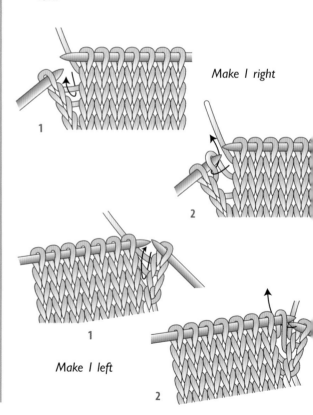

Make 1 right

Make 1 left

12

CABLES

- 6-Stitch Cable Twisted to the Right (C6B): Place the next 3 stitches on an extra needle held behind the work, knit the next 3 stitches, then knit the 3 stitches from the extra needle.
- 6-Stitch Cable Twisted to the Left (C6F): Place the next 3 stitches on an extra needle or cable needle held in front of the work, knit the next 3 stitches, then knit the 3 stitches from the extra needle.

Work the stitches of the cable in stockinette stitch for the next 5 rows, and work the cable twist every 6th row.

6-stitch cable twisted to the right

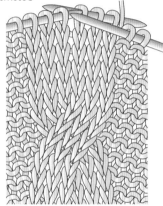

6-stitch cable twisted to the left

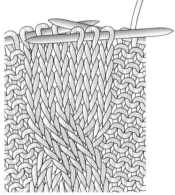

BUTTONHOLES

The yarn over is ideal for making a buttonhole. It will form a little hole that you can put a button through. Work stitches to where you want the buttonhole, yarn over, then work 2 stitches together (1). In the next row, work the yarn over like a normal stitch (2).

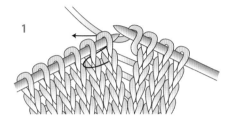

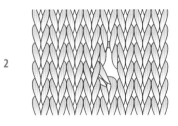

13

PICKING UP STITCHES

With a needle, pick up all the stitches along an edge.

- If working an edge with bound-off stitches: insert the needle through each bound-off stitch. Once all the stitches are on the needle, knit them normally to form the first row, and so on.
- If working a garter stitch edge (the side edge of a knitted piece): insert the needle through each edge stitch that forms part of a garter-stitch ridge; once all the stitches are on the needle, knit the first row.
- If working "live" stitches set aside on a needle, simply slip them—without knitting them—onto the new needle.

CASTING ON ADDITIONAL STITCHES (KNITTED CAST-ON)

At the beginning of a row, knit 1 stitch. Place the stitch obtained on the right needle back onto the left needle: you have added 1 stitch. Knit it and place the stitch obtained on the right needle back onto the left needle, and so on, until you have the number of stitches needed.

14

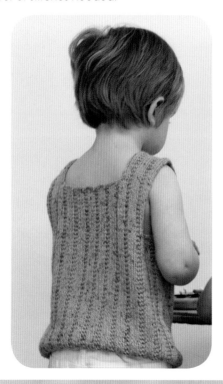

BINDING OFF STITCHES

Knit the first two stitches, then insert the left needle into the first stitch and pass this stitch over the second one (1). Knit a third stitch and use the left needle to pass the first stitch on the right needle over the new stitch. Continue, working 1 stitch at a time and passing the previous stitches over the new ones as you go (2). At the end of the row, you will have 1 stitch left; cut the yarn, pass the end through this stitch, and pull gently to fasten off.

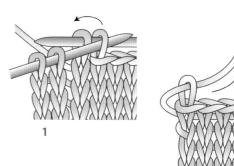

1

2

ASSEMBLING EDGES TOGETHER

To assemble a project neatly with an invisible seam, iron the pieces first to flatten out the edges well. Place them side by side, with the right sides facing you, and insert a threaded yarn needle under the strand on the side of the first edge stitch of the first piece, then under the strand on the side of the first edge stitch of the other piece. Pull gently to bring the two pieces together to obtain an invisible seam. Continue in this way until the seam is complete.

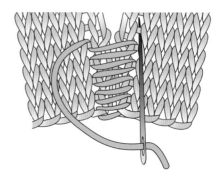

3-NEEDLE BIND-OFF FOR SHOULDER SEAMS

Sewing shoulder seams together is not always easy and can be difficult to accomplish neatly. Once you master this method, you'll never go back! When you finish knitting each piece, set it aside with the stitches still live on the needles.

To assemble the shoulder of a back piece and a front piece: place the two pieces together, with right sides together and the needles pointing in the same direction. Take a third needle of the same size and knit the first shoulder stitch of the back together with the first shoulder stitch of the front; the stitch formed should be placed on the third needle. With this third needle, again knit 1 stitch of the front together with a back stitch, placing it on the third needle. You will have 2 stitches on the third needle; bind off one of these stitches by passing the first stitch over the second one. Continue to knit the shoulder stitches together, binding them off from the third needle as you go. At the end, you will have 1 stitch left; cut the yarn and pass the end through this stitch, and pull gently to close the loop. The shoulder is assembled and the seam is just as neat on both sides!

BLOCKING YOUR WORK

When a piece is completed, blocking it will give it a nice finish. The piece will be gently flattened and certain stitches highlighted, such as edges or cables. Iron all the pieces on the wrong side on low heat. If some of the edges tend to roll up, iron them a second time on the right side, very gently, then assemble the piece.

NEEDLE BUTTON LOOP (A WAY OF MAKING A BUTTONHOLE)

Attach the yarn firmly on the edge, making sure the join isn't visible. Create 2 or 3 loops of the same size by inserting the needle through the knitted work several times, and fasten off the last loop securely. Bring the yarn through the middle of this loop, then insert the needle through the loop that was just formed, and pull to tighten. Continue until the end of the loop, and fasten off the last loop securely at the edge of the piece.

Crochet Lesson

CHAIN STITCH (CH)

Make a slip knot and place it on the crochet hook (1). Bring the yarn over the hook from back to front, catch the working yarn with the hook (2), and pull it through the slip knot, forming a new loop (3). Yarn over again from back to front and bring the yarn through the loop just created, and continue in this fashion until you've obtained a chain of the desired length.

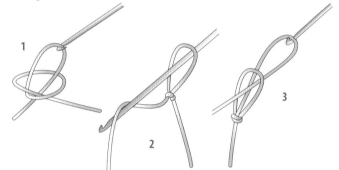

SLIP STITCH (SL ST)

On a base chain, insert the hook through the second stitch from the hook. Yarn over and pull the loop formed through the chain stitch and through the first loop on the hook. Repeat this step along the chain, inserting the hook into each chain stitch to obtain a complete row of slip stitch.

SINGLE CROCHET (SC)

Start as for a slip stitch. Yarn over and pull the yarn only through the chain stitch (1). Yarn over again and pull this loop through the first yarn over and through the first loop on the hook. You should have 1 loop remaining (2). Repeat these two steps all along the row.

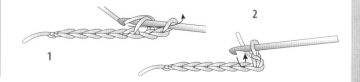

Knitting for our little ones is easy!

And what a joy to see them wear our creations!

1 . . . 2 . . . 3 . . . knit!

Raglan Pullover

The pretty raspberry color and the cute bow tie add to the charm of this bubbly pullover!

SIZES
❊ 2 (4, 6) years

MATERIALS
❊ 100% wool light weight yarn: 5 (5, 6) skeins raspberry (shown in Pierrot Pure Wool DK; 1.7 oz./50 g; 80 yd./ 73 m; Framboise)
❊ U.S. size 6 (4 mm) and 7 (4.5 mm) needles

STITCHES USED
❊ Stockinette stitch (see p. 9)
❊ Whimsical ribbing:
  Row 1 and all odd rows (WS): *P2, k2; repeat from * to end.
  Even rows: *P1, k2, p1, sl 1 pwise wyif, p1, yo, pass slipped stitch over p1 and yo; repeat from * to end.

GAUGE
❊ In whimsical ribbing, on size 6 needles: 26 sts x 32 rows = 4 x 4 in./10 x 10 cm
❊ In stockinette stitch, on size 7 needles: 21 sts x 26 rows = 4 x 4 in./10 x 10 cm

BACK
With size 6 needles, cast on 80 (86, 92) sts and knit 1 row, then—starting on the wrong side—work whimsical ribbing pattern for 2.75 (3, 3.5) in./7 (8, 9) cm. Continue in stockinette stitch with size 7 needles until the piece measures 8 (9, 9.5) in./20 (22, 24) cm in all. Bind off the first stitch of the next 2 rows, then start raglan decreases 2 sts from the edge of each RS row, 13 (14, 15) times in all, as follows: k2, sk2p, knit to last 5 sts, k3tog, k2. Bind off the remaining 26 (28, 30) sts.

FRONT
Work like the back until the armholes.
After the third raglan decrease row, 66 (72, 78) sts remain. Divide the work into 2 halves and continue to work on the 33 (36, 39) stitches of the left side. Continuing the raglan decreases on the outside edge, create a V neck by decreasing 1 st at the end of every RS row: at the end of the row, when 3 sts remain, k2tog, then k1, 10 (11, 12) times in all. Bind off the 3 remaining sts.
Pick up the 33 (36, 39) sts of the right front and, still continuing the raglan decreases on the outside edge, work (k1, skp) at the beginning of each RS row for the V neck, 10 (11, 12) times in all. Bind off the 3 remaining sts.

SLEEVES
With the size 7 needles, cast on 72 (76, 82) sts and work in stockinette stitch. After the third row, work a 1-stitch decrease, 1 st from the edge of each RS row (5 times): k1, k2tog, knit to last 3 sts, skp, k1—62 (66, 72) sts remaining. Bind off 1 st at the beginning of each of the next 2 rows, then begin the raglan decreases as for the back/front, 13 (14, 15) times in all. Bind off the 8 (8, 10) remaining sts.

FINISHING
Sew the sides and the raglan edges together.
To make the bow tie, cast on 12 sts and work in stockinette stitch for 6 in./16 cm, then bind off. Fold the piece into a rectangle and sew the 3 open sides together. Tie the center of this piece tightly to form a bow tie and wrap the yarn around it several times to hold the shape. Sew the bow tie to the bottom of the V neck of the pullover.

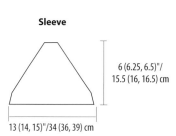

Sleeve

6 (6.25, 6.5)"/ 15.5 (16, 16.5) cm

13 (14, 15)"/34 (36, 39) cm

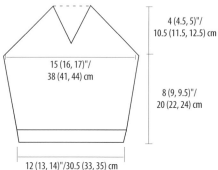

Front and Back

4 (4.5, 5)"/ 10.5 (11.5, 12.5) cm

15 (16, 17)"/ 38 (41, 44) cm

8 (9, 9.5)"/ 20 (22, 24) cm

12 (13, 14)"/30.5 (33, 35) cm

Boy's Pullover with Rolled Edges

For today's little daredevils: an ultra-comfortable, super-soft pullover.

SIZES

❊ 2 (4, 6) years

MATERIALS

❊ Wool-alpaca blend medium weight yarn: 5 (6, 6) skeins mauve and 2 (2, 2) skeins green (shown in Bouton d'Or Cocoon; 1.7 oz./50 g; 82 yd./75 m; Taupe and Verdi)

❊ U.S. size 7 (4.5 mm) and 6 (4 mm) straight needles for the buttoned straps and U.S. size 7 (4.5 mm) circular needles

❊ Four .5 in./15 mm buttons

STITCHES USED

❊ Garter stitch (see p. 9)
❊ Stockinette stitch (see p. 9)

GAUGE

❊ In stockinette stitch, on size 7 needles: 20 sts x 26 rows = 4 x 4 in./10 x 10 cm

BACK

Cast on 64 (68, 72) sts with green and work in stockinette stitch for 16 (18, 20) rows. Continue in mauve until the piece measures 9.5 (10.75, 12) in./24 (27, 30) cm in all. Bind off the first 2 sts of the next 2 rows, then begin the raglan decreases 2 sts from the end of each RS row: 2 sts 3 times (at the beginning of the row, k2, then k3tog; at the end of the row, when 5 sts remain, sk2p, k2), then 1 st 12 (13, 14) times (at the beginning of the row, k2, k2tog; at the end of the row, when 4 sts remain, skp, k2). Set the remaining 24 (26, 28) sts aside.

FRONT

Work like the back to the raglan shaping, and until there are 32 (34, 36) sts remaining.

For the collar: While continuing the raglan decreases, k9 and set aside; bind off the next 14 (16, 18) sts and knit the remaining 9. Bind off 1 st on the collar side, then 1 st 2 rows later (continuing the raglan decreases). Set the remaining 3 sts aside. Pick up the 9 sts you set aside earlier and repeat the same decrease pattern in reverse.

SLEEVES

Cast on 42 (46, 50) sts in green and work 6 rows of stockinette stitch. Continue in stockinette stitch in mauve, increasing 1 st, 1 st from the edge, at each end of a RS row when the piece measures 3 (3.5, 4) in./8 (9, 10) cm, and again at 6 (7, 8) in./16 (18, 20) cm. You will have 46 (50, 54) sts. Continue until the piece measures 9 (10.75, 12) in./24 (27, 30) cm in all, then bind off the first 2 sts of the next 2 rows (starting with a RS row). Work the raglan decreases as for the back/front, that is: 2 sts, 2 sts from the edge, 3 times, then 1 st, 2 sts from the edge, 12 (13, 14) times. Set aside the remaining 6 (8, 10) sts. Make a second sleeve the same as the first.

FINISHING

Iron the pieces, leaving a rolled edge at the bottom. Sew the side seams, the bottoms of the sleeves, and the raglan seams (for a nice finish, sew the rolled-up parts in place from the wrong side; see p. 31).

For the collar, use the circular needle (knit the collar in the round without seams, or in rows, placing the seam between the back and a sleeve): take up the 24 (26, 28) sts of the back, then the 6 (8, 10) sts of 1 sleeve, then pick up 30 (32, 34) sts along the front collar, then take up the 6 (8, 10) sts of the other sleeve. Work 6 rows of stockinette stitch in green, then bind off.

For the buttoned straps: With green and size 6 needles, pick up 5 sts on the WS in the middle of a sleeve, at the sixth row, and work 52 rows in garter stitch (this will be 26 ridges), then bind off the stitches. Make a second strap, and sew 1 button onto each strap and 2 on the collar where the raglan seams meet it.

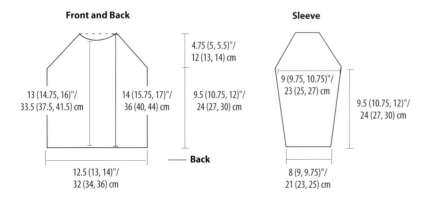

Front and Back

4.75 (5, 5.5)"/12 (13, 14) cm

13 (14.75, 16)"/33.5 (37.5, 41.5) cm

14 (15.75, 17)"/36 (40, 44) cm

9.5 (10.75, 12)"/24 (27, 30) cm

Back

12.5 (13, 14)"/32 (34, 36) cm

Sleeve

9 (9.75, 10.75)"/23 (25, 27) cm

9.5 (10.75, 12)"/24 (27, 30) cm

8 (9, 9.75)"/21 (23, 25) cm

Ruffled Dress

A fun play dress with ruffles, little buttons, and a retro look!

SIZES
✼ 2 (4, 6) years

MATERIALS
✼ Cotton-rayon blend fine weight yarn: 5 (6, 6) skeins eggplant (shown in Bouton d'Or Mango; 1.7 oz./50 g; 120 yd. /110 m; Grappe)
✼ U.S. size 4 (3.5 mm) needles
✼ Yarn needle
✼ Seven .5 in./11 mm buttons
✼ 1 stitch holder

STITCHES USED
✼ Stockinette stitch (see p. 9)
✼ Garter stitch (see p. 9)

GAUGE
✼ In stockinette stitch, on size 4 needles: 22 sts x 30 rows = 4 x 4 in./10 x 10 cm

BACK

Cast on 160 (168, 176) sts and work in stockinette stitch for 2 (2, 2.75) in./6 (6, 7) cm. On a RS row, bind off every other stitch—80 (84, 88) sts remaining. Continue in stockinette stitch.

When the piece measures 6 (7, 8) in./16 (18, 20) cm total, begin decreasing: on a RS row, knit 2 sts together 12 sts from each edge; repeat every 8 rows until 5 decrease rows have been worked—70 (74, 78) sts remaining. Work even until the piece measures 15.75 (16.5, 17.25) in./40 (42, 44) cm. Bind off 4 sts on each edge for the armholes—62 (66, 70) sts remaining. On the next RS row, begin decreasing for the armholes: knit 2 sts together, 1 st from the edge, at the beginning of each row (RS and WS), 7 times—48 (52, 56) sts remaining. When the piece measures 20 (21.25, 22.5) in./51 (54, 57) cm, knit the next 12 (13, 14) sts, set them aside, bind off the center 24 (26, 28) sts, and knit the remaining 12 (13, 14) sts. Bind off 1 st at the beginning of the next RS row (on the collar side of the piece), work another 3 rows, then set the remaining 11 (12, 13) sts aside. Pick up the 12 (13, 14) sts of the left shoulder and work them in mirror image of the right side, then set the remaining 11 (12, 13) sts aside.

FRONT

Start as for the back; after the decreases 12 sts from the edge, 70 (74, 78) sts remain. Separate the piece into two parts: work 33 (35, 37) sts, then set the next 37 (39, 41) sts aside. Cast on 4 sts at the end of the 33 (35, 37) sts just knit; work these stitches in garter stitch for the rest of the piece, to create the button band.

When the piece measures 15.75 (16.5, 17.25) in./40 (42, 44) cm, bind off 4 sts at the beginning of a RS row for the armhole; then work the armhole decreases by knitting 2 sts together, 1 st from the edge, 7 times—26 (28, 30) sts remaining. When the piece measures 18 (19, 20) in./46 (49, 51) cm, bind off 11 (12, 13) sts on the collar edge (that is, at the beginning of a WS row) once, then bind off 1 st at the beginning of every other row, 4 times. Continue on the remaining 11 (12, 13) sts until the piece measures 20.5 (21.75, 23) in./52 (55, 58) cm, then set the stitches aside.

Take up the 37 (39, 41) sts of the second half of the front and work the first 4 sts in garter stitch for the button band. As you work this half of the dress, make 7 buttonholes (k2, yo, k2tog) in the button band, the first one .4 (.6, .6) in./1 (1.5, 1.5) cm above the beginning of the button band, and the following buttonholes spaced 1 in./3 cm apart. Work the sleeve and collar decreases as for the left side of the front (but reversed).

FINISHING

Attach the front and back shoulders together using the 3-needle bind-off method (see p. 15). Iron the 2 pieces on low heat, then sew the side seams and the bottom of the button band on the wrong side. Sew the 7 buttons on the left side of the button band, under the buttonholes.

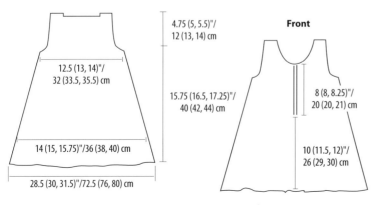

Back

12.5 (13, 14)"/ 32 (33.5, 35.5) cm

14 (15, 15.75)"/36 (38, 40) cm

28.5 (30, 31.5)"/72.5 (76, 80) cm

4.75 (5, 5.5)"/ 12 (13, 14) cm

15.75 (16.5, 17.25)"/ 40 (42, 44) cm

Front

8 (8, 8.25)"/ 20 (20, 21) cm

10 (11.5, 12)"/ 26 (29, 30) cm

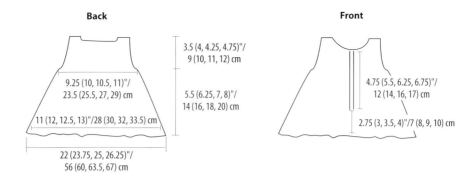

Back

3.5 (4, 4.25, 4.75)"/ 9 (10, 11, 12) cm

9.25 (10, 10.5, 11)"/ 23.5 (25.5, 27, 29) cm

5.5 (6.25, 7, 8)"/ 14 (16, 18, 20) cm

11 (12, 12.5, 13)"/28 (30, 32, 33.5) cm

22 (23.75, 25, 26.25)"/ 56 (60, 63.5, 67) cm

Front

4.75 (5.5, 6.25, 6.75)"/ 12 (14, 16, 17) cm

2.75 (3, 3.5, 4)"/7 (8, 9, 10) cm

SIZES
❋ *3 (6, 12, 18) months*

MATERIALS
❋ *Cotton-rayon blend fine weight yarn: 2 (2, 3, 3) skeins orange (shown in Bouton d'Or Mango; 1.7 oz./50 g; 120 yd./110 m; Japonais)*
❋ *U.S. size 4 (3.5 mm) needles*
❋ *Yarn needle*
❋ *4 (4, 5, 5) .5 in./11 mm buttons*
❋ *1 stitch holder*

STITCHES USED
❋ *Stockinette stitch (see p. 9)*

GAUGE
❋ *In stockinette stitch, with size 4 needles: 22 sts x 30 rows = 4 x 4 in./10 x 10 cm.*

RUFFLED TUNIC
BACK
Cast on 124 (132, 140, 148) sts and work in stockinette stitch for 1.5 (1.5, 2, 2) in./4 (4, 5, 5) cm. On a RS row, bind off every other stitch—62 (66, 70, 74) sts remaining. Continue in stockinette stitch.

When the piece measures 2.25 (2.75, 3, 3.5) in./6 (7, 8, 9) cm total, begin decreasing: on a RS row, knit 2 sts together 10 sts from each edge; repeat every 2 (2, 4, 4) rows until 5 decrease rows have been worked—52 (56, 60, 64) sts remaining.

Work even until the piece measures 5.5 (6.25, 7, 8) in./14 (16, 18, 20) cm. Bind off 3 sts on each edge for the sleeve holes—46 (50, 54, 58) sts remaining. On the next RS row, begin decreasing for the armholes: knit 2 sts together, 1 st from the edge, at the beginning of each row (RS and WS), 7 times—32 (36, 40, 44) sts remaining. When the piece measures 8.5 (10, 10.25, 12) in./22 (25, 26, 31) cm, knit the next 8 (9, 10, 11) sts, set them aside, bind off the next 16 (18, 20, 22) sts, and knit the remaining 8 (9, 10, 11) sts. Bind off 1 st at the beginning of the next RS row (on the collar side of the piece); purl 1 more row, then set the remaining 7 (8, 9, 10) sts aside. Pick up the 8 (9, 10, 11) sts of the left shoulder and work them in mirror image of the right side, then set the remaining 7 (8, 9, 10) sts aside.

FRONT
Work as for the back until 2 rows below the first decrease after the ruffle—that is, when the piece measures 2.75 (3, 3.5, 4) in./7 (8, 9, 10) cm total—60 (64, 68, 72) sts. Separate the piece into two parts, as follows: work 28 (30, 32, 34) sts, then

set the next 32 (34, 36, 38) sts aside. Cast on 4 sts at the end of the 28 (30, 32, 34) sts just knit for the button band; work these stitches in garter stitch (knit every row) throughout. Continue on these 32 (34, 36, 38) sts, working the decrease 10 sts from the edge as for the back. When the piece measures 5.5 (6.25, 7, 8) in./14 (16, 18, 20) cm total, bind off 3 sts at the beginning of a RS row; next work the armhole decreases by knitting 2 sts together 1 st from the edge, 7 times—18 (20, 22, 24) sts remaining. When the piece measures 7.5 (8.5, 10, 10.5) in./19 (22, 25, 27) cm in all, bind off 8 (9, 10, 10) sts on the collar edge (that is, at the beginning of a WS row) once, then bind off 1 st at the beginning of every other row, 3 (3, 3, 4) times. Continue on the remaining 7 (8, 9, 10) sts until the piece measures 23 (26, 29, 32) sts, then set the stitches aside.

Take up the 32 (34, 36, 38) sts of the second half of the front and work the first 4 sts in garter stitch for the button band. As you work this half of the dress—working the decrease 10 sts from the edge—work 4 (4, 5, 5) buttonholes (k2, yo, k2tog) in the button band, the first one .3 in./1 cm above the beginning of the button band, and the following buttonholes spaced 1 (1.25, 1.25, 1.5) in./3 (3.5, 3.5, 4) cm apart. Work the sleeve and collar decreases as for the left side of the front (but reversed).

FINISHING
Attach the front and back shoulders together using the 3-needle bind-off (see p. 15). Iron the 2 pieces on low heat, then sew the side seams and sew on the 4 (4, 5, 5) buttons.

Summer Pocket Pullover

A very nomad chic look for your dapper young fellow!

SIZES
❋ 2 (4, 6) years

MATERIALS
❋ Wool-cotton blend medium weight yarn: 2 (3, 3) hanks ecru (shown in Spud & Chloë Sweater; 3.5 oz./100 g; 160 yd./146 m; Ice Cream)
❋ U.S. size 8 (5 mm) needles
❋ Yarn needle
❋ Stitch holders

STITCHES USED
❋ Garter stitch (see p. 9)
❋ Stockinette stitch (see p. 9)

GAUGE
❋ In stockinette stitch, on size 8 needles: 18 sts x 24 rows = 4 x 4 in./10 x 10 cm.

BACK

Cast on 57 (61, 65) sts and work 10 rows in garter stitch. Continue in stockinette stitch until the piece measures 9 (10, 10.5) in./23 (25, 27) cm, then begin the raglan decreases, 3 sts from the edge, as follows: at the beginning of the row, k3, then k3tog; at the end of the row, when 6 sts remain, sk2p, k3. (Note: Always knit the 3 edge stitches, whether the row is a knit row or a purl row, in order to create a garter-stitch armhole border.)

Repeat these double decreases on every RS row, 6 times in all—33 (37, 41) sts remaining. Work even, still knitting the 3 edge stitches at the beginning and end of every row, until the piece measures 14 (15, 16.5) in./36 (39, 42) cm total. Bind off the first 8 (9, 10) sts and the last 8 (9, 10) sts, setting the center 17 (19, 21) sts aside.

FRONT

Work as for the back until the end of the armhole decreases—33 (37, 41) sts remaining. Separate the piece into two parts: work the first 14 (16, 18) sts and set the remaining 19 (21, 32) sts aside. Cast on 5 more stitches on the collar edge of these 14 (16, 18) sts (these 5 sts will be knit every row, just like the 3 sts on the armhole edge). Work even until the piece measures 14 (15, 16.5) in./36 (39, 42) cm total, then bind off the first 8 (9, 10) sts on the shoulder edge and set the 11 (12, 13) collar sts aside. Take up the 19 (21, 23) sts of the other half of the front and work them in the same way as the first half, but in mirror image.

FINISHING

Sew the front and back shoulders together. Put the 11 (12, 13) sts of the right collar together with the 17 (19, 21) sts of the back collar, and the 11 (12, 13) sts of the left collar: you will have 39 (43, 47) sts in all. Work even in garter stitch for 12 rows, then bind off loosely. Gently iron the entire piece, then sew the side seams.

Garter stitch pocket: Pick up 30 (32, 34) sts on the center of the front, about 3 (3.5, 4) in./8 (9, 10) cm above the bottom edge, and work 6 rows even in garter stitch. Continue in garter stitch, decreasing 1 st, 2 sts from the edge, by knitting 2 sts together at the beginning of every RS and WS row, 6 times—18 (20, 22) sts remaining. Work even for another 6 (8, 10) rows, then bind off. Sew the top edge of the pocket to the sweater with invisible stitches.

Front and Back

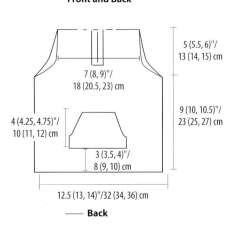

5 (5.5, 6)"/ 13 (14, 15) cm

7 (8, 9)"/ 18 (20.5, 23) cm

9 (10, 10.5)"/ 23 (25, 27) cm

4 (4.25, 4.75)"/ 10 (11, 12) cm

3 (3.5, 4)"/ 8 (9, 10) cm

12.5 (13, 14)"/32 (34, 36) cm

—— **Back**

Asymmetrical Cardigan

A well-shaped cardigan made of soft yarn will allow little ones freedom in all their movements. Make one for each special girl you know. The pattern includes a wide range of sizes—even a doll size!

❋ Juniors Small (Medium, Large)

MATERIALS
❋ Wool-blend medium weight yarn: 6 (7, 8) skeins ecru (shown in Cascade Cash Vero; 1.7 oz./50 g; 98 yd./90 m; Ecru)
❋ U.S. size 6 (4 mm) circular needles
❋ 1 brooch
❋ Yarn needle
❋ Stitch holders
❋ 8 ring-style stitch markers

STITCH USED
❋ Stockinette stitch (see p. 9)

GAUGE
❋ In stockinette stitch, on size 6 needles: 22 sts x 30 rows = 4 x 4 in./10 x 10 cm.

FOR BIG KIDS
YOKE
This project is worked in a single piece, starting from the collar.

Cast on 128 (138, 148) sts and work 8 rows in stockinette stitch. On the ninth row, spread out 30 (32, 34) increases as follows: k6 (7, 8), (inc, k4) 30 (32, 34) times, k2 (3, 4)—158 (170, 182) sts. On the next WS row, place the 8 stitch markers as follows: p41 (43, 45), pm, p1, pm, p25 (27, 29), pm, p1, pm, p42 (46, 50), pm, p1, pm, p25 (27, 29), pm, p1, pm, p21 (23, 25).

On the next RS row, begin the sleeve increases by increasing by 1 st before and after each group of 2 markers (that is, 8 increases per row) on every RS row, 23 (24, 25) times in all: k21 (23, 25), inc, sm, k1, sm, inc, k25 (27, 29), inc, sm, k1, sm, inc, k42 (46, 50), inc, sm, k1, sm, inc, k25 (27, 29), inc, sm, k1, sm, inc, k41 (43, 45).

After all the increases are completed, you should have the following number of stitches: 44 (47, 50) sts, marker, 1 st, marker, 71 (75, 79) sts, marker, 1 st, marker, 88 (94, 100) sts, marker, 1 st, marker, 71 (75, 79) sts, marker, 1 st, marker, 64 (67, 70) sts.

SLEEVES
Work the 45 (48, 51) sts of the first front, then set them aside on a stitch holder. Continue on the 71 (75, 79) sts of the first sleeve, setting aside the 90 (96, 102) sts of the back, the 71 (75, 79) sts of the second sleeve, and 65 (68, 71) sts of the second front on a second stitch holder. On the first sleeve sts, work even until the sleeve measures 13.75 (14.5, 15.25) in./35 (37, 39) cm from the armhole, then bind off. Take up the 71 (75, 79) sts of the second sleeve and work them in the same way.

BODY
Take up the 45 (48, 51) sts of the first front and at the same time put them together with the 90 (96, 102) sts of the back and the 65 (68, 71) sts of the second front—200 (212, 224) sts in all. Work even until the piece measures 12 (13, 14) in./30 (33, 36) cm from the armholes, then bind off.

FINISHING
Iron the piece on gentle heat, leaving a rolled edge of .3 in/1 cm around the collar and at the ends of the sleeves and the bottom of the body. Sew up the sleeves, making sure to begin sewing on the wrong side about .3 in./1 cm from the ends of the sleeves, so that the seam is not visible on the outside of the rolled edge. Close the cardigan with a brooch.

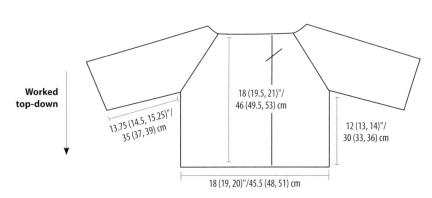

Worked top-down

13.75 (14.5, 15.25)" / 35 (37, 39) cm

18 (19.5, 21)" / 46 (49.5, 53) cm

12 (13, 14)" / 30 (33, 36) cm

18 (19, 20)"/45.5 (48, 51) cm

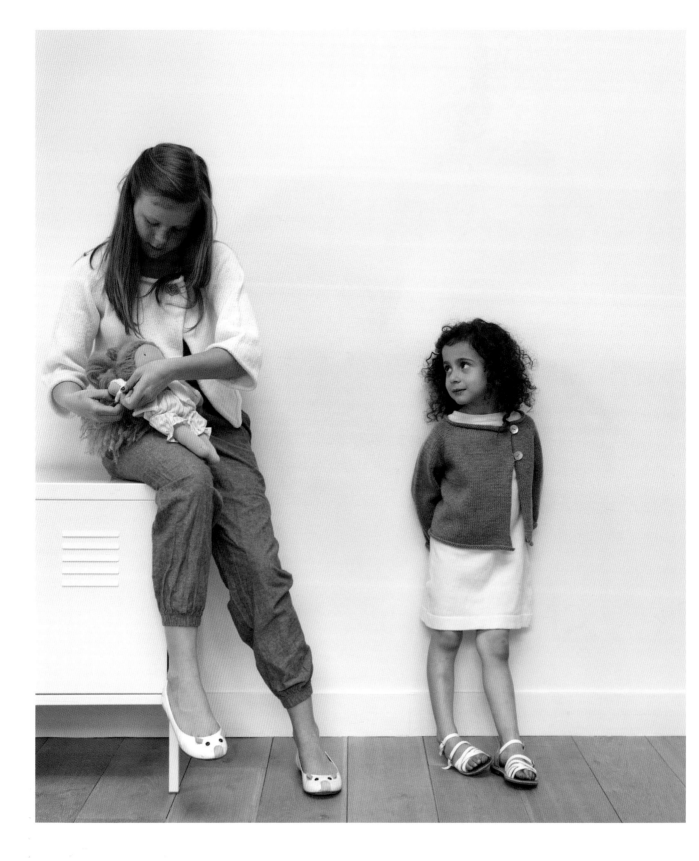

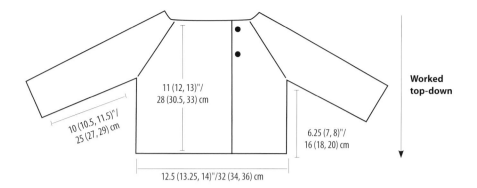

11 (12, 13)"/ 28 (30.5, 33) cm

10 (10.5, 11.5)"/ 25 (27, 29) cm

6.25 (7, 8)"/ 16 (18, 20) cm

Worked top-down

12.5 (13.25, 14)"/32 (34, 36) cm

FOR LITTLE GIRLS
YOKE
This project is worked in a single piece, starting from the collar.

Cast on 80 (88, 96) sts and work 6 rows in stockinette stitch. On the seventh row, spread out 18 (20, 22) increases as follows: k6, (inc, k4) 18 (20, 22) times, k2—98 (108, 118) sts. On the next WS row, place the 8 stitch markers as follows: p29 (31, 33), pm, p1, pm, p13 (15, 17), pm, p1, pm, p30 (32, 34), pm, p1, pm, p13 (15, 17), pm, p1, pm, p9 (11, 13). On the next RS row, begin the sleeve increases by increasing by 1 st before and after each group of 2 markers (that is, 8 increases per row) on every RS row, 17 (18, 19) times in all: k9 (11, 13), inc, sm, k1, sm, inc, k13 (15, 17), inc, sm, k1, sm, inc, k30 (32, 34), inc, sm, k1, sm, inc, k13 (15, 17), inc, sm, k1, sm, inc, k29 (31, 33).

After all the increases are completed, you should have the following number of stitches: 26 (29, 32) sts, marker, 1 st, marker, 47 (51, 55) sts, marker, 1 st, marker, 64 (68, 72) sts, marker, 1 st, marker, 47 (51, 55) sts, marker, 1 st, marker, 46 (49, 52) sts.

SLEEVES
Work the 27 (30, 33) sts of the first front, then set them aside on a stitch holder. Continue on the 47 (51, 55) sts of the first sleeve, setting aside the 66 (70, 74) sts of the back, the 47 (51, 55) sts of the second sleeve, and 47 (50, 53) sts of the second front on a second stitch holder.

On the first sleeve sts, work even for 4.75 (5, 5.5) in./12 (13, 14) cm, then work 1 decrease 1 st from the edge at the beginning and end of a RS row—45 (49, 53) sts remaining. Work even until the sleeve measures 10 (10.5, 11.5) in./25 (27, 29) cm from the armhole, then bind off. Take up the 47 (51, 55) sts of the second sleeve and work them in the same way.

BODY
Take up the 27 (30, 33) sts of the first front and at the same time put them together with the 66 (70, 74) sts of the back and the 47 (50, 53) sts of the second front, removing all the stitch markers as you do so—140 (150, 160) sts in all. Work even until the piece measures 6.25 (7, 8) in./16 (18, 20) cm from the armholes, then bind off.

FINISHING
Iron the piece on gentle heat, leaving a rolled edge of .3 in./1 cm around the collar and at the ends of the sleeves and the bottom of the body. Sew up the sleeves, making sure to begin sewing on the wrong side about .3 in./1 cm from the ends of the sleeves, so that the seam is not visible on the outside of the rolled edge. Add two button loops (see p. 15), the first one .75 in./2 cm below the collar, and the second one 2 (2.75, 3) in./6 (7, 7.5) cm lower. Sew on the two buttons opposite the button loops.

SIZES

❊ *Chest: 12.5 (16.5) in./32 (42) cm*

MATERIALS

❊ *Wool-bamboo blend fine weight yarn: 1 skein ecru (shown in Cheval Blanc Bamboulène; 1.7 oz./50 g; 120 yd./110 m; Ecru)*
❊ *U.S. size 4 (3.5 mm) needles*
❊ *One .5 in./15 mm button*
❊ *Yarn needle*
❊ *Stitch holders*
❊ *8 ring-style stitch markers*

STITCH USED

❊ *Stockinette stitch (see p. 9)*

GAUGE

❊ *In stockinette stitch, on size 4 needles: 24 sts x 36 rows = 4 x 4 in./10 x 10 cm.*

FOR DOLLS
YOKE

This project is worked in a single piece, starting from the collar.

Cast on 48 (58) sts and work 4 rows in stockinette stitch. On the fifth row, spread out 10 increases as follows: k2, (k4 (5), inc) 10 times, k6—58 (68) sts. On the next WS row, place the 8 stitch markers as follows: p8 (10), pm, p1, pm, p6 (8), pm, p1, pm, p19 (21), pm, p1, pm, p6 (8), pm, p1, pm, p15 (17). On the next RS row, begin the sleeve increases by increasing by 1 st before and after each group of 2 markers (that is, 8 increases per row) on every RS row, 8 (9) times in all: k15 (17), inc, sm, k1, sm, inc, k6 (8), inc, sm, k1, sm, inc, k19 (21), inc, sm, k1, sm, inc, k6 (8), inc, sm, k1, sm, inc, k8 (10).

After all the increases are completed, you should have the following number of stitches: 23 (26) sts, marker, 1 st, marker, 22 (26) sts, marker, 1 st, marker, 35 (39) sts, marker, 1 st, marker, 22 (26) sts, marker, 1 st, marker, 16 (19) sts.

SLEEVES

Work the 23 (26) sts of the first front, then set them aside on a stitch holder. Continue on the 24 (28) sts of the first sleeve, setting aside the 35 (39) sts of the back, the 24 (28) sts of the second sleeve, and 16 (19) sts of the second front on a second stitch holder. On the first sleeve sts, work even until the sleeve measures 2 (2.75) in./5 (7) cm from the armhole, then bind off. Take up the 24 (28) sts of the second sleeve and work them in the same way.

BODY

Take up the 23 (26) sts of the first front and at the same time put them together with the 35 (39) sts of the back and the 16 (19) sts of the second front—74 (84) sts in all. Work even until the piece measures 2.25 (3) in./6 (8) cm from the armholes, then bind off.

FINISHING

Iron the piece on gentle heat, leaving a rolled edge of .25 in./0.5 cm around the collar and at the ends of the sleeves and the bottom of the body. Sew up the sleeves (see the instructions in the little girls size). Add a button loop (see p. 15) on the right side, .3 in./1 cm below the collar. Sew on the button opposite the button loop.

Rolled-Edge Pullover

Slip into summer with this practical pullover, knitted in a lovely bright red cotton. Add quirky little details, such as buttons and ribbons, to give it even more personality.

SIZES
❋ 2 (4, 6) years

MATERIALS
❋ 100% cotton bulky weight yarn: 6 (6, 7) skeins poppy red (shown in Cheval Blanc Nomade; 1.7 oz./50 g; 55 yd./50 m; Coquelicot)
❋ U.S. size 7 (4.5 mm) straight needles and U.S. size 7 (4.5 mm) circular needles (for the collar)
❋ Two .75 in./18 mm buttons
❋ 8 in./20 cm of novelty ribbon

STITCH USED
❋ Stockinette stitch (see p. 9)

GAUGE
❋ In stockinette stitch, on size 7 needles: 17 sts x 23 rows = 4 x 4 in./10 x 10 cm.

BACK
Cast on 54 (58, 62) sts and knit even until the piece measures 9.5 (10.75, 12) in./24 (27, 30) cm. Bind off the first 2 sts of the next 2 rows (starting with a RS row), then begin the raglan decreases, 2 sts from the edge of the piece, at the beginning of each row: decrease 2 sts, 3 times (at the beginning of each RS row, k2, sk2p; at the beginning of each WS row, p2, p3tog), then decrease 1 st 9 (10, 11) times (at the beginning of each RS row, k2, skp; at the beginning of each WS row, p2, p2tog). Set the remaining 20 (22, 24) sts aside.

FRONT
Cast on 54 (58, 62) sts and work as for the back through the raglan decreases, until 26 (28, 30) sts remain. For the collar, bind off the 12 (14, 16) center stitches (continuing the raglan decreases). Set the 6 sts of the right aside and continue on the 7 sts of the left side (the seventh stitch will be removed at the beginning of the next row, when you work the raglan decrease). Continue on this side, binding off 1 st on the collar side of the piece twice (still continuing the raglan decreases). Bind off the 2 remaining sts and work the right side the same way, but in mirror image.

SLEEVES
Cast on 40 (44, 48) sts and work 6 rows of stockinette stitch, then bind off 2 sts at each edge and begin the raglan decreases, 2 sts from the edge, as for the back/front, that is: 2 sts at the beginning of each row, 3 times, then 1 st at the beginning of each row, 9 (10, 11) times. Set the remaining 6 (8, 10) sts aside. Work the second sleeve in the same way.

FINISHING
Iron the pieces on gentle heat, leaving the rolled edges. Sew the side seams, the bottom seams of the sleeves, and the raglan seams (for a nice finish, sew the seam on the rolled edge on the WS, see page 31). For the collar, use the circular needle (you can work the collar in the round, without seams, or back and forth in rows, sewing the ends of the rows together where the back and one sleeve meet): take up the 20 (22, 24) sts of the back, then the 6 (8, 10) sts of one sleeve, then pick up 22 (24, 26) sts around the front collar edge, then take up the 6 (8, 10) sts of the second sleeve. Work 6 rows of stockinette stitch, then bind off.

Front and Back

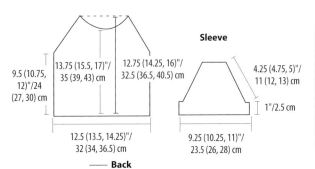

9.5 (10.75, 12)"/24 (27, 30) cm

13.75 (15.5, 17)"/ 35 (39, 43) cm

12.75 (14.25, 16)"/ 32.5 (36.5, 40.5) cm

12.5 (13.5, 14.25)"/ 32 (34, 36.5) cm

—— **Back**

Sleeve

4.25 (4.75, 5)"/ 11 (12, 13) cm

1"/2.5 cm

9.25 (10.25, 11)"/ 23.5 (26, 28) cm

IDEA
Cut 4 in./10 cm of ribbon, fold it in half, and place it around the border of the front; attach it in place with a button sewed over the end. Do the same thing at the level of the neck.

Little Striped Cardi

Go for a pretty couture look with this cardigan knitted in a single piece from the bottom up.

SIZES
✻ 2 (4, 6) years

MATERIALS
✻ Wool-alpaca blend fine weight yarn: 2 (3, 3) skeins pink and 1 (2, 2) skeins brown (shown in Bergère de France Lima; 1.7 oz./ 50 g; 120 yd./110 m; Aurore and Maquis)
✻ U.S. size 4 (3.5 mm) circular needles
✻ Yarn needle
✻ Three .5 in./15 mm buttons

STITCHES USED
✻ Stockinette stitch (see p. 9)
✻ Reverse stockinette stitch (see p. 9)
✻ Garter stitch (see p. 9)

GAUGE
✻ In stockinette stitch, with size 4 needles: 22 sts x 32 rows = 4 x 4 in./10 x 10 cm.

BOTTOM
Cast on 134 (144, 154) sts with pink and knit 6 rows in garter stitch, then alternate 2 rows stockinette stitch in brown with 2 rows of garter stitch in pink, twice. Continue in stockinette stitch in pink until the piece measures 7 (8, 8.75) in./18 (20, 22) cm. Separate the piece into 3 sections: 35 (37, 40) sts for the first front, 64 (70, 74) sts for the back, and 35 (37, 40) sts for the second front. Set the sts aside.

SLEEVES
Cast on 46 (50, 54) sts with pink and work 4 rows in garter stitch, then set aside. Work a second sleeve in the same way.

YOKE
On a RS row, put the sleeves and the body of the cardigan together as follows: with pink, knit the 35 (37, 40) sts of the first front, then the 46 (50, 54) sts of the first sleeve, then the 64 (70, 74) sts of the back, then the 46 (50, 54) sts of the second sleeve, and finally the 35 (37, 40) sts of the second front—226 (244, 262) sts. Work another row of knit, then alternate 2 rows stockinette stitch in brown and 2 rows of garter stitch in pink, 4 (5, 6) times.

On the fifth (sixth, seventh) stripe of stockinette stitch (in brown), work the knit row; then, on the purl row, work 34 (36, 38) decreases, distributed as follows: p13 (16, 19), p2tog, (p4, p2tog) 33 (35, 37) times, p13 (16, 19)—192 (208, 224) sts remaining.

Work another 2 rows garter stitch in pink, 2 rows stockinette stitch in brown, 2 rows garter stitch in pink, and 2 rows stockinette stitch in brown. On the final row of the second brown stripe, work 34 (36, 38) decreases, distributed as follows: p12 (15, 18), p2tog, (p3, p2tog) 33 (35, 37) times, p13 (16, 19)—158 (172, 186) sts remaining.

Again, work another 2 rows garter stitch in pink, 2 rows stockinette stitch in brown, 2 rows garter stitch in pink, and 2 rows stockinette stitch in brown. On the final row of the second brown stripe, work 34 (36, 38) decreases, distributed as follows: p12 (15, 18), p2tog, (p2, p2tog) 33 (35, 37) times, p12 (15, 18)—124 (136, 148) sts remaining.

Work one more set of 2 rows garter stitch in pink, 2 rows stockinette stitch in brown, 2 rows garter stitch in pink, and 2 rows stockinette stitch in brown. On the final row of the second brown stripe, work 38 (42, 46) decreases, distributed as follows: p5, p2tog, (p1, p2tog) 37 (41, 45) times, p6—86 (94, 102) sts remaining. Work another 2 rows of garter stitch in pink and 2 rows of stockinette stitch in brown, then finish with 6 rows of garter stitch in pink. Bind off the 86 (94, 102) sts.

FINISHING
Sew the small bottom seams of the sleeves. With pink yarn, pick up about 2 sts for every 3 rows along the left front edge and knit 6 rows of garter stitch, then bind off. Repeat on the right side, working (on the third row) 3 buttonholes (yo, k2tog), the first one placed 3 sts below the collar, then the others below it, with all the buttonholes spaced 10 (12, 12) sts apart. Sew 3 buttons opposite on the button band on the left side.

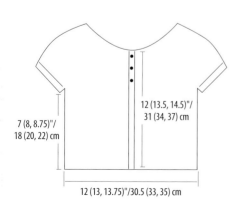

12 (13.5, 14.5)"/ 31 (34, 37) cm

7 (8, 8.75)"/ 18 (20, 22) cm

12 (13, 13.75)"/30.5 (33, 35) cm

MATERIALS

❊ *Wool-alpaca blend fine*
   weight yarn: I skein pink
   and I skein brown (shown in
   Bergère de France Lima;
   1.7 oz./50 g;120 yd./110 m;
   Aurore and Maquis)

❊ *U.S. size 4 (3.5 mm)*
   needles

❊ *Yarn needle*

❊ *Four .5 in./15 mm buttons*

GAUGE

❊ *In stockinette stitch, on size*
   4 needles: 22 sts x 32 rows
   = 4 x 4 in./10 x 10 cm.

LITTLE MATCHING PURSE
BODY

With the pink yarn, cast on 80 sts, then
   work 8 rows of garter stitch.

Continue in stockinette stitch until the
   piece measures 2.5 in./6 cm in all. Work
   2 rows garter stitch, then with brown,
   2 rows of stockinette stitch. Continue
   alternating between 2 rows of garter
   stitch in pink and 2 rows of stockinette
   stitch in brown until the piece measures 5 in./12 cm in all, then bind off.

HANDLES

With pink yarn, cast on 80 sts. Work 6 rows
   of garter stitch, then bind off. Make
   the second handle in the same way.

FINISHING

Iron the large rectangle on gentle heat,
   then fold it in half. Sew up the side and
   bottom of the bag. Place the ends of
   the handles on garter stitch part of the
   bag (on the inside), about 1 in./2.5 cm
   from each end. Sew them in place,
   sewing a button on the outside of the
   bag over each handle end and adding
   a few extra stitches on the inside to
   keep the handles in place.

Sleeveless Tweed Vest

The pretty tweed wool gives this super-simple vest a nice drape and a chic allure.

SIZES
❋ 2 (4, 6) years

MATERIALS
❋ Wool-acrylic-rayon blend tweed medium weight yarn: 4 (5, 6) skeins raspberry (shown in Plassard Tweed; 1.7 oz./50 g; 137 yd./125 m; #N102)
❋ U.S. size 8 (5.0 mm) needles
❋ Yarn needle
❋ One .75 to 1 in./18 to 22 mm button
❋ Stitch holder

STITCH USED
❋ Garter stitch (see p. 9)

GAUGE
❋ In garter stitch, with two strands of yarn held together, on size 8 needles: 17 sts x 34 rows = 4 x 4 in./10 x 10 cm.

FOR BIG KIDS
BOTTOM
Working with two strands of yarn held together throughout, cast on 37 (40, 44) sts and work in garter stitch for 25 (26.75, 28.25) in./64 (68, 72) cm (that is, 100, 106, 112 ridges). You will obtain a rectangle that will form the bottom part of the vest.

TOP
Back yoke: On the longest side of the rectangle, pick up 46 (48, 50) sts in the center; starting on the next row, decrease by 1 st (by knitting 2 sts together), 2 sts from the edge, at the beginning of the next RS and WS rows, 6 times total—34 (36, 38) sts remaining. Work even until the piece measures 5 (5.5, 6) in./13 (14, 15) cm, then set the sts aside.

Right front yoke: Pick up 24 (26, 28) sts on the first part of the rectangle and decrease 1 st at the beginning of each WS row (2 sts from the edge), 6 times—18 (20, 22) sts remaining. Work even until the piece measures 3.5 (4, 4.5) in./9 (10, 11) cm from the bottom of this section, then begin the collar decreases: bind off 5 (6, 7) sts at the beginning of the next RS row, then bind off 1 st at the beginning of the next 3 RS rows. Work even on the remaining 10 (11, 12) sts until the piece measures 5 (5.5, 6) in./13 (14, 15) cm from the bottom of this section, then set the sts aside. Work the left front yoke in mirror image.

FINISHING
Put the sts for the back and fronts back on the needles and, using the 3-needle bind-off (see p. 15), knit the 10 (11, 12) sts of the left front together with the first 10 (11, 12) sts of the back, binding them off as you go; next bind off the 14 (14, 14) central back sts, and finally knit together and bind off the remaining 10 (11, 12) back sts with the 10 (11, 12) sts of the right front.

For the girl version, add a button loop (see p. 15) to the right side, at the edge of the collar. Sew the button opposite on the left front. Invert the positions of the button (left side) and button loop (right side) for the boy version.

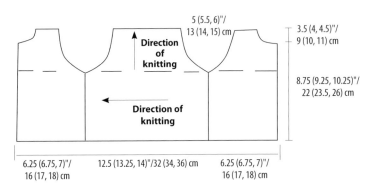

5 (5.5, 6)"/ 13 (14, 15) cm

3.5 (4, 4.5)"/ 9 (10, 11) cm

Direction of knitting

Direction of knitting

8.75 (9.25, 10.25)"/ 22 (23.5, 26) cm

6.25 (6.75, 7)"/ 16 (17, 18) cm   12.5 (13.25, 14)"/32 (34, 36) cm   6.25 (6.75, 7)"/ 16 (17, 18) cm

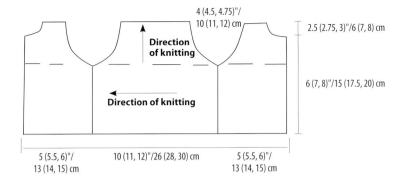

4 (4.5, 4.75)"/
10 (11, 12) cm

Direction of knitting

2.5 (2.75, 3)"/6 (7, 8) cm

Direction of knitting

6 (7, 8)"/15 (17.5, 20) cm

5 (5.5, 6)"/
13 (14, 15) cm

10 (11, 12)"/26 (28, 30) cm

5 (5.5, 6)"/
13 (14, 15) cm

SIZES
❉ 6 (12, 18) months

MATERIALS
❉ Wool-acrylic-rayon blend tweed medium weight yarn: 4 (4, 4) skeins green (shown in Plassard Tweed; 1.7 oz./50 g; 137 yd./125 m; #880)
❉ U.S. size 8 (5.0 mm) needles
❉ Yarn needle
❉ One .75 in./18 mm button
❉ Stitch holder

STITCH USED
❉ Garter stitch (see p. 9)

GAUGE
❉ In garter stitch, with two strands of yarn held together, on size 8 needles: 17 sts x 34 rows = 4 x 4 in./10 x 10 cm.

FOR LITTLE ONES
BOTTOM

Working with two strands of yarn held together throughout, cast on 26 (30, 34) sts and work in garter stitch for 20.5 (22, 23.75) in./52 (56, 60) cm (that is, 82, 88, 94 ridges). You will obtain a rectangle that will form the bottom part of the vest.

TOP

Back yoke: On the longest side of the rectangle, pick up 38 (40, 42) sts in the center; starting on the next row, decrease by 1 st (by knitting 2 sts together), 2 sts from the edge, at the beginning of the next RS and WS rows, 6 times total—26 (28, 30) sts remaining. Work even until the piece measures 4 (4.5, 4.75) in./10 (11, 12) cm, then set the sts aside.

Right front yoke: Pick up 19 (21, 23) sts on the first part of the rectangle and decrease 1 st at the beginning of each WS row (2 sts from the edge), 6 times—13 (15, 17) sts remaining. Work even until the piece measures 2.5 (2.75, 3) in./6 (7, 8) cm from the bottom of this section, then begin the collar decreases: bind off 3 (4, 5) sts at the beginning of the next RS row, then bind off 1 st at the beginning of the next 3 RS rows. Work even on the remaining 7 (8, 9) sts until the piece measures 4 (4.5, 4.75) in./10 (11, 12) cm from the bottom of this section, then set the sts aside. Work the left front yoke in mirror image.

FINISHING

Put the sts for the back and the two fronts back on the needles and, using the 3-needle bind-off (see p. 15), knit the 7 (8, 9) sts of the left front together with the first 7 (8, 9) sts of the back, binding them off as you go; next bind off the 12 (12, 12) central back sts, and finally knit together and bind off the remaining 7 (8, 9) back sts with the 7 (8, 9) sts of the right front.

For the girl version, add a button loop (see p. 15) to the right side, at the edge of the collar. Sew the button opposite on the left front. Invert the positions of the button (left side) and button loop (right side) for the boy version.

Pumpkin Spice Cardigan

This cardigan is easy to wear and easy to match for an elegant little look.

SIZES
❋ 2 (4, 6) years

MATERIALS
❋ Wool-alpaca blend light weight yarn: 3 (3, 4) skeins brown and 2 (2, 2) skeins orange (shown in Cheval Blanc Quito; 1.7 oz./50 g; 109 yd./100 m; Chataigne and Paprika)
❋ U.S. size 6 (4 mm) and 7 (4.5 mm) needles
❋ U.S. size 7 (4.5 mm) circular needles
❋ U.S. size G-6 (4 mm) crochet hook
❋ 8 ring-style stitch markers
❋ Five .5 in./15 mm buttons

STITCHES USED
❋ Stockinette stitch (see p. 9)
❋ 1x1 ribbing (see p. 10)

GAUGE
❋ In stockinette stitch, on size 7 needles: 18 sts x 25 rows = 4 x 4 in./10 x 10 cm.

BODY
With the size 6 needles and brown yarn, cast on 118 (126, 134) sts and work in 1x1 ribbing for 2 (2.25, 2.5) in./5 (5.5, 6) cm. Continue in stockinette stitch on the size 7 needles, alternating 2 rows of brown and 2 rows of orange, until the piece measures 9 (10, 10.75) in./23 (25, 27) cm. Separate the piece into 3 sections—right front, 31 (33, 35) sts; back, 56 (60, 64) sts; and left front, 31 (33, 35) sts—and set aside.

SLEEVES
With the size 6 needles and brown yarn, cast on 44 (48, 52) sts and work in 1x1 ribbing for 1.75 (2, 2.25) in./4.5 (5, 5.5) cm. Continue in stockinette stitch on the size 7 needles, alternating 2 rows of brown and 2 rows of orange until the piece measures 8.75 (9.5, 10.25) in./22 (24, 26) cm. Set aside and knit a second sleeve.

RAGLAN SECTION
The sleeves and body should end with stripes of the same color; if not, add the two rows of the missing color to the body so that the pieces match up.

Put the body and sleeves together on the circular needles, starting with the right front (31, 33, 35 sts), then the right sleeve (44, 48, 52 sts), the back (56, 60, 64 sts), the left sleeve (44, 48, 52 sts), and finally the left front. With brown yarn, start the raglan decreases: k29 (31, 33), k2tog, pm, k1, pm, skp, k38 (42, 46), k2tog, pm, k1, pm, skp, k52 (56, 60), k2tog, pm, k1, pm, skp, k38 (42, 46), k2tog, pm, k1, pm, skp, k29 (31, 33).

Repeat these 8 decreases (before and after every set of two stitch markers) on the next 13 (14, 15) RS rows; after the last decrease row, you should have the following: 18 (19, 20) sts, marker, 1 st, marker, 16 (18, 20) sts, marker, 1 st, marker, 30 (32, 34) sts, marker, 1 st, marker, 16 (18, 20) sts, marker, 1 st, marker, 18 (19, 20) sts—102 (110, 118) sts in all.

Remove the stitch markers and place the work back on the size 6 needles. On the next RS row, work 20 decreases, distributed as follows: k3 (7, 11), (k2tog, k3) 19 times, k2tog, k2 (6, 10)—82 (90, 98) sts. On the next RS row, continue in 1x1 ribbing. On the third ribbing row, work 20 (22, 24) yos: k2, (yo, k2tog) 20 (22, 24) times. Bind off on the sixth ribbing row.

NOTE
This design is worked in a single piece, starting from the bottom; the only sewing needed is the bottom sleeve seams.

FINISHING

Weave in the ends and sew the sleeve seams. With the size 6 needles, pick up 102 (108, 114) sts along the right front edge. Work 6 rows of 1x1 ribbing, working 6 buttonholes (yo, k2tog) in the third row, placing the first after the second stitch from the top of the piece, and spacing the others 8 (10, 10) sts apart. Make a second border along the left side, only making one button-hole (in the third row, after the second stitch from the top). With the size G-6 crochet hook, make a chain 1 yd./1 m long and thread it through the eyelets on the collar and the 2 top button-holes. Sew the 5 buttons opposite the 5 lower buttonholes.

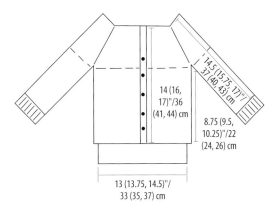

14 (16, 17)"/36 (41, 44) cm

14.5 (15.75, 17)"/37 (40, 43) cm

8.75 (9.5, 10.25)"/22 (24, 26) cm

13 (13.75, 14.5)"/33 (35, 37) cm

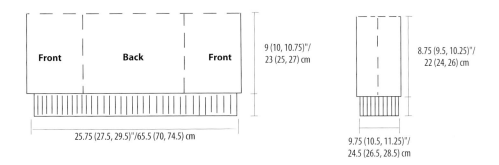

Front   **Back**   **Front**

9 (10, 10.75)"/23 (25, 27) cm

25.75 (27.5, 29.5)"/65.5 (70, 74.5) cm

8.75 (9.5, 10.25)"/22 (24, 26) cm

9.75 (10.5, 11.25)"/24.5 (26.5, 28.5) cm

Cool Tank

A vintage style modernized by a simple graphic design and beautiful, radiant wool. Little and big kids will love it!

SIZES

❋ 2 (4, 6) years

MATERIALS

❋ Wool-acrylic-rayon blend tweed medium weight yarn: 2 (3, 3) skeins sky blue (shown in Plassard Tweed; 1.7 oz./ 50 g; 137 yd./125 m; #209)
❋ U.S. size 4 (3.5 mm) needles
❋ Yarn needle
❋ Stitch holders

STITCHES USED

❋ Stockinette stitch (see p. 9)
❋ Whimsical 3x2 ribbing (see p. 10)

GAUGE

❋ In whimsical 3x2 ribbing, on size 4 needles: 23 sts x 32 rows = 4 x 4 in./10 x 10 cm.

FRONT AND BACK

This design is knitted in a single piece, starting on the front.

Cast on 73 (78, 83) sts and work in whimsical 3x2 ribbing until the piece measures 6 (6.25, 6.75) in./15 (16, 17) cm. From this point, work the first 25 sts in 3x2 ribbing, the next 23 (28, 33) sts in stockinette stitch, and the remaining 25 sts in 3x2 ribbing; continue in this pattern until the piece measures 8.5 (9.5, 10.25) in./22 (24, 26) cm. Next, bind off 10 sts at each edge for the armholes—53 (58, 63) sts remaining. Continue, working all sts in 3x2 ribbing, until the piece measures 11.5 (12, 13.25) in./29 (31, 34) cm. For the head hole, work 13 sts, then bind off the center 27 (32, 37) sts, and work the remaining 13 sts; continue on just these 13 sts for 4.25 (4.75, 5) in./11 (12, 13) cm.

Set the 13 sts of the right shoulder aside and take up the 13 sts of the left shoulder. Work in 3x2 ribbing for 4.25 (4.75, 5) in./11 (12, 13) cm, then cast on 27 (32, 37) sts, and finally take up the 13 sts of the right shoulder. You should have 53 (58, 63) sts again.

Work in 3x2 ribbing for 7 (7, 8) cm to form the other side of the armhole area, then add 10 sts at each side—73 (78, 83) sts. Work even until the piece measures 8.5 (9.5, 10.25) in./22 (24, 26) cm from the end of the armholes, then bind off.

FINISHING

Iron the pieces on low heat to flatten the sides. Sew the sides of the tank top, and, if you like, decorate the stockinette section in the front—embroidery, initials, or a decorative patch would look great.

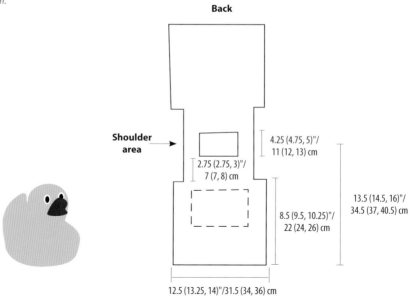

Back

Shoulder area →

2.75 (2.75, 3)"/ 7 (7, 8) cm

4.25 (4.75, 5)"/ 11 (12, 13) cm

13.5 (14.5, 16)"/ 34.5 (37, 40.5) cm

8.5 (9.5, 10.25)"/ 22 (24, 26) cm

12.5 (13.25, 14)"/31.5 (34, 36) cm

Front

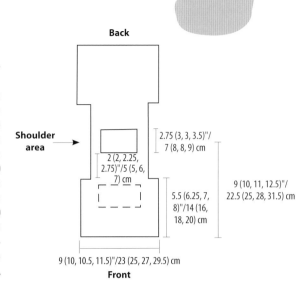

BABY BOY VARIATION
FRONT AND BACK

This design is knitted in a single piece, starting on the front.

Cast on 53 (58, 63, 68) sts and work in whimsical 3x2 ribbing until the piece measures 2.75 (3, 3.5, 4.25) in./7 (8, 9, 11) cm. From this point, work the first 20 sts in 3x2 ribbing, the next 13 (18, 23, 28) sts in stockinette stitch, and the remaining 20 sts in 3x2 ribbing; continue in this pattern until the piece measures 5.5 (6.25, 7, 8) in./14 (16, 18, 20) cm. Next, bind off 10 sts at each edge for the armholes—33 (38, 43, 48) sts remaining. Continue, working all sts in 3x2 ribbing, until the piece measures 7.5 (8.25, 9.5, 10.5) in./19 (21, 24, 27) cm.

For the head hole, work 8 (10, 10, 10) sts, then bind off the center 17 (18, 23, 28) sts, and work the remaining 8 (10, 10, 10) sts; continue on just these sts for 2.75 (3, 3, 3.5) in./7 (8, 8, 9) cm.

Set the sts of the right shoulder aside and take up the 8 (10, 10, 10) sts of the left shoulder. Work in 3x2 ribbing for 2.75 (3, 3, 3.5) in./7 (8, 8, 9) cm, then cast on 17 (18, 23, 28) sts, and finally take up the 8 (10, 10, 10) sts of the right shoulder. You should have 33 (38, 43, 48) sts again.

Work in 3x2 ribbing for 2, (2, 2.25, 2.75) in./5 (5, 6, 7) cm to form the other side of the armhole area, then add 10 sts at each side—53 (58, 63, 68) sts. Work even until the piece measures 5.5 (6.25, 7, 8) in./14 (16, 18, 20) cm from the end of the armholes, then bind off.

FINISHING

Iron the pieces on low heat to flatten the sides. Sew the sides of the tank top, and decorate the stockinette section in the front—embroidery, initials, or a decorative patch would look great.

Back

Shoulder area →

2.75 (3, 3, 3.5)"/ 7 (8, 8, 9) cm

2 (2, 2.25, 2.75)"/5 (5, 6, 7) cm

5.5 (6.25, 7, 8)"/14 (16, 18, 20) cm

9 (10, 11, 12.5)"/ 22.5 (25, 28, 31.5) cm

9 (10, 10.5, 11.5)"/23 (25, 27, 29.5) cm

Front

Bright Bolero

This little jacket is truly adorable, with its colored stripes and its soft cotton yarn! It's comfortable enough to wear right on the skin.

SIZES
✻ 2 (4, 6) years

MATERIALS
✻ 100% cotton fine weight yarn: 1 skein each in orange, lime green, yellow, dark green, red, and blue (shown in DMC Natura Just Cotton; 1.7 oz./ 50 g; 170 yd./155 m; Coral, Pistache, Tournesol, Green Valley, Passion, and Star Light)
✻ U.S. size 4 (3.5 mm) circular needles
✻ Yarn needle
✻ Five .5 in./12 mm buttons
✻ 8 ring-style stitch markers
✻ Stitch holder

STITCHES USED
✻ Stockinette stitch (see p. 9)
✻ Seed stitch (see p. 10)

GAUGE
✻ In stockinette stitch, on size 4 needles: 24 sts x 32 rows = 4 x 4 in./10 x 10 cm.

BODY
This design is worked in a single piece, starting from the collar. Change colors every 2 rows, with red being the main color.

With red yarn, cast on 118 (128, 138) sts and work 2 rows in seed stitch. On the third row, continue in stockinette stitch with dark green for the main piece, keeping a border of 4 sts in seed stitch in red on each end of the piece.

At the same time, at the end of the third row, when 4 sts remain, work a buttonhole: yo, k2tog, k1, p1. Space out the other 4 buttonholes 1.5 (2, 2.25) in./4 (5, 6) cm apart along the button band. Also on this same row, begin the increases, as follows: work 23 (25, 27) sts, inc, pm, k1, pm, inc, k17 (19, 21), inc, pm, k1, pm, inc, k34 (36, 38), inc, pm, k1, pm, inc, k17 (19, 21), inc, pm, k1, pm, inc, work remaining 23 (25, 27) sts. Repeat this pattern of increases on every RS row, 17 (18, 19) times total, to obtain the following stitch count: 40 (43, 46) sts, marker, 1 st, marker, 51 (55, 59) sts, marker, 1 st, marker, 68 (72, 76) sts, marker, 1 st, marker, 51 (55, 59) sts, marker, 1 st, marker, 40 (43, 46) sts. Remove the markers.

SLEEVES
Work the 41 (44, 47) sts of the front, set them aside, then continue on the 51 (55, 59) sts of the first sleeve (setting the sts of the back, second sleeve, and second front aside as well).

Work 4 rows of seed stitch in red, then bind off. Work the 70 (74, 78) sts of the back, then set them aside and continue on the 51 (55, 59) sts of the second sleeve. Work the second sleeve the same as the first one.

Pick up the 41 (44, 47) sts of the second front and finish the row. Putting the back and the fronts together again, you should have 152 (162, 172) sts. Without forgetting the 4-st seed stitch border, work even in stockinette st until the piece measures 3 (4.75, 6) in./8.5 (12, 15.5) cm from the armholes, then change back to red and work 6 rows of seed stitch (that is, about .5 in./1.5 cm). Bind off.

FINISHING
Iron the work on low heat and sew the seams at the bottoms of the sleeves. Weave in the ends. Sew the 5 buttons to the button band opposite the buttonholes.

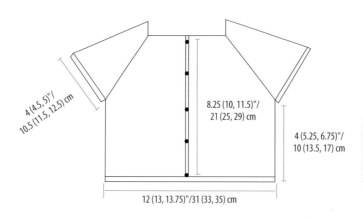

4 (4.5, 5)"/ 10.5 (11.5, 12.5) cm

8.25 (10, 11.5)"/ 21 (25, 29) cm

4 (5.25, 6.75)"/ 10 (13.5, 17) cm

12 (13, 13.75)"/31 (33, 35) cm

TIP
When you change color in the middle of a row, make sure to cross the yarns over each other to avoid an embarrassing hole!

Sweetest Layette Set

Make it in a very elegant gray for a chic baby.

SIZES

❋ 3 (6, 12, 18) months

MATERIALS

❋ Wool-alpaca blend fine
  weight yarn: 2 (2, 3, 3) skeins
  pearl gray for the cardigan
  and 1 (1, 1, 2) skein(s) pearl
  gray for the bonnet (shown
  in Bergère de France Lima;
  1.7 oz./50 g; 120 yd./110 m;
  Gris Perle)
❋ U.S. size 4 (3.5 mm) circular
  needles (for the cardigan),
  U.S. size 4 (3.5 mm) straight
  needles (for the bonnet)
❋ Yarn needle
❋ Four .5 in/15 mm buttons
❋ 8 ring-style stitch markers

STITCHES USED

❋ Stockinette stitch (see p. 9)
❋ Alternate seed stitch (see
  p. 10)

GAUGE

❋ In stockinette stitch, on size
  4 needles: 23 sts x 30 rows
  = 4 x 4 in./10 x 10 cm.

CARDIGAN

This design is worked in a single piece, starting from the collar.

Cast on 76 (82, 88, 94) sts and work 12 rows in alternate seed stitch. At the same time, at the end of the third row, make 1 buttonhole: when 4 sts remain, yo, k2tog, k1, p1. Space out the other 2 buttonholes 1.75 (2, 2.25, 2.5) in./4.5 (5, 5.5, 6) cm apart.

Starting on the thirteenth row, continue in stockinette stitch, keeping a border of 4 sts of alternate seed stitch at the beginning and end of each row; work 60 (66, 72, 78) increases, distributed as follows: work 4 sts in seed stitch, k4, (k1, inc) 60 (66, 72, 78) times, k4, work 4 sts in seed stitch—136 (148, 160, 172) sts. Work even for 6 (8, 10, 12) rows. On the next RS row, work 8 increases, distributed as follows: work 23 (25, 27, 29) sts, inc, pm, k1, pm, inc, k24 (26, 28, 30), inc, pm, k1, pm, inc, k38 (42, 46, 50), inc, pm, k1, pm, inc, k24, (26, 28, 30), inc, pm, k1, pm, inc, work remaining 23 (25, 27, 29) sts. Repeat this pattern of increases on every RS row, 7 (8, 9, 10) times total, to obtain the following stitch count: 30 (33, 36, 39) sts, marker, 1 st, marker, 38 (42, 46, 50) sts, marker, 1 st, marker, 52 (58, 64, 70) sts, marker, 1 st, marker, 38 (42, 46, 50) sts, marker, 1 st, marker, 30 (33, 36, 39) sts. Remove the markers.

For the sleeves, work the 31 (34, 37, 40) sts of the front, set them aside, and continue in stockinette stitch on the 38 (42, 46, 50) sts of the first sleeve (setting aside the sts of the back, second sleeve, and second front). When the sleeve measures 4.75 (5.5, 6.25, 7) in./12 (14, 16, 18) cm from the armhole, continue for .75 in./2 cm in alternate seed stitch, then bind off. Work the 54 (60, 66, 72) sts of the back, then set them aside and continue on the 38 (42, 46, 50) sts of the second sleeve. Work this sleeve the same as the first sleeve. Take up the 31 (34, 37, 40) sts of the second front and finish the row. Putting the back and the fronts together, you should have 116 (128, 140, 152) sts. Without forgetting the seed stitch border, work even on these stitches in stockinette stitch until the piece measures 4.75 (5.5, 6.25, 7) in./12 (14, 16, 18) cm from the armhole, then work in alternate seed stitch for 1 in./2.5 cm. Bind off.

FINISHING

Iron the piece on low heat, and sew up the bottom seams of the sleeves. Sew the 3 buttons on the button band, opposite the buttonholes.

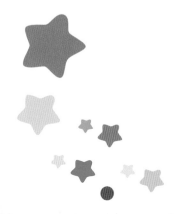

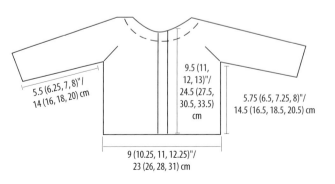

5.5 (6.25, 7, 8)"/
14 (16, 18, 20) cm

9.5 (11, 12, 13)"/
24.5 (27.5, 30.5, 33.5) cm

5.75 (6.5, 7.25, 8)"/
14.5 (16.5, 18.5, 20.5) cm

9 (10.25, 11, 12.25)"/
23 (26, 28, 31) cm

BONNET

Cast on 90 (94, 98, 102) sts and work in alternate seed stitch for 1.5 (1.5, 2, 2) in./4 (4, 5, 5) cm.

Continue in stockinette stitch until the piece measures 3 (3.25, 3.5, 4) in./7.5 (8, 9, 10) cm, then begin decreasing on every RS row, as follows (purling each st on the WS rows):

K1, (k19 (20, 21, 22), k3tog) 4 times, k1—82 (86, 90, 94) sts.

K1, (k17 (18, 19, 20), k3tog) 4 times, k1—74 (78, 82, 86) sts.

K1, (k15 (16, 17, 18), k3tog) 4 times, k1—66 (70, 74, 78) sts.

Continue to decrease in this pattern on the RS rows, until you work the row: k1, (k1 (2, 3, 4), k3tog) 4 times, k1—10 (14, 18, 22) sts.

For 12 and 18 months only: Work one more row, working each pair of sts together—9 (11) sts.

FINISHING

Thread the yarn through the 10 (14, 9, 11) remaining sts, and pull tight to fasten off. Sew the side seam. Sew on the button.

57

Cabled Set

An ultra-comfortable sweater to keep your little ones nice and warm.
Make the hat and leg warmers to match, for a really adorable look!

SIZES
❋ 2 (4, 6) years

MATERIALS (SWEATER)
❋ 100% wool bulky weight yarn:
1 (1, 2) hanks dark gray
(shown in Cascade Ecological
Wool; 8.8 oz./250 g;
478 yd./437 m; Antique)
❋ Five 1 in./22 mm buttons
❋ U.S. size 9 (5.5 mm) and 10
(6 mm) straight needles
❋ U.S. size 10 (6 mm) circular
needle
❋ U.S. size 10 (6 mm) cable
needle (or double-pointed
needle)
❋ Stitch holder

STITCHES USED
❋ Stockinette stitch (see. p 9)
❋ Whimsical ribbing:
Row 1 (and all odd rows):
*K2, p1; repeat from * across.
**Row 2 (and all even
rows):** Purl.
❋ Cables twisted to the left
(C6F) and right (C6B) (see
p. 13)

GAUGE
❋ In stockinette stitch, on size
10 needles: 18 sts x 22 rows
= 4 x 4 in./10 x 10 cm.

CARDIGAN
BOTTOM

With the size 9 needles, cast on 128 (137, 146) sts and work in whimsical ribbing for 1.5 in./4 cm, ending the odd-numbered rows with two knits. Continue on size 10 needles in stockinette stitch and cables (8 in all): k2, p1, k2, p2, C6B, p2, k3 (4, 4), p2, C6B, p2, k10 (13, 17), p2, C6B, p2, k4, p2, C6B, p2, k4 (5, 6), p2, C6F, p2, k4, p2, C6F, p2, k10 (13, 17), p2, C6F, p2, k3 (4, 4), p2, C6F, p2, k2, p1, k2. At the same time, work the first buttonhole 2.75 (3, 3.5) in./7 (8, 9) cm from the bottom of the piece, at the beginning of the row (k2, yo, k2tog) for girls and at the end of the row (when 4 sts remain, k2tog, yo, k2) for boys; space out the remaining buttonholes 2.25 (2.5, 2.75) in./6 (6.5, 7) cm apart.

When the cables measure 4.75 (5, 5.5) in./12 (13, 14) cm, stop working cables 2, 3, 6, and 7 (counting cables in the order in which you knit them across a row—see photo) and continue in stockinette stitch on these stitches.

When the piece measures 9 (10, 10.5) in./23 (25, 27) cm in all, stop working cables 1, 4, 5, and 8 and separate the work into 3 pieces: 33 (35, 38) sts for the fronts and 62 (67, 70) sts for the back.

TOP

Work 32 (34, 37) sts (first front), set the stitches aside, and bind off the next 2 sts. Continue on the 60 (65, 68) sts of the back and set the remaining 34 (36, 39) sts aside.

Back: On the next RS row, start the double raglan decreases, 2 sts from each edge: k2, k3tog, then at the end of the row, when 5 sts remain, sk2p, k2. Repeat these decreases on each RS row, 3 times total. Continue with single decreases, as follows: k2, k2tog; at the end of the row, when 4 sts remain, skp, k2; work these decreases on each RS row, 10 (11, 12) times. Set the remaining 28 (31, 32) sts aside.

Left front: Take back up the 34 (36, 39) sts of the second front and bind off the first 2 sts. At the beginning of each RS row, work the double or single raglan decreases as for the back. When 19 (20, 22) sts remain, bind off the collar edge (still continuing the raglan decreases on the other edge): bind off 1 st, 8 (9, 10) times, then bind off 3 sts twice. Then bind off the 2 (2, 3) remaining sts.

Right front: Take up the 32 (34, 37) sts of the first front and work the raglan decreases at the end of each RS row. Bind off the collar sts as for the left front, in mirror image. Bind off the 2 (2, 3) remaining sts.

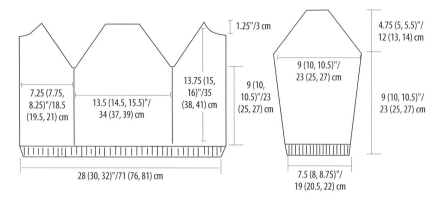

Schematic measurements

Body (left panel):
- 7.25 (7.75, 8.25)"/18.5 (19.5, 21) cm
- 13.5 (14.5, 15.5)"/34 (37, 39) cm
- 13.75 (15, 16)"/35 (38, 41) cm
- 9 (10, 10.5)"/23 (25, 27) cm
- 1.25"/3 cm
- 28 (30, 32)"/71 (76, 81) cm

Sleeve (right panel):
- 4.75 (5, 5.5)"/12 (13, 14) cm
- 9 (10, 10.5)"/23 (25, 27) cm
- 9 (10, 10.5)"/23 (25, 27) cm
- 7.5 (8, 8.75)"/19 (20.5, 22) cm

MATERIALS
(LEG WARMERS)

❋ *100% wool bulky weight yarn: 1 (1, 2) hanks dark gray (shown in Cascade Ecological Wool; 8.8 oz./250 g; 478 yd./437 m; Antique)*

❋ *U.S. size 9 (5.5 mm) and 10 (6 mm) straight needles*

❋ *U.S. size H-8 (5 mm) crochet hook*

SLEEVES

With the size 9 needles, cast on 34 (37, 40) sts and work in whimsical ribbing for 1.5 in./4 cm. Continue on the size 10 needles in stockinette stitch and cables: k12 (13, 15), p2, C6B, p2, k12 (14, 15). Don't forget to twist the cable every 6 rows! At the same time, work 1 Make 1 increase 1 st from the edge, at the beginning and end of a RS row when the piece measures 2 (2.75, 3.5) in./5 (7, 9) cm, 3.75 (4.5, 5.25) in./9.5 (11.5, 13.5) cm, 5.5 (6.25, 7) in./14 (16, 18) cm, and 7.25 (8, 9) in./18.5 (20.5, 22.5) cm. You will have 42 (45, 48) sts.

When the piece measures 9 (10, 10.5) in./23 (25, 27) cm, bind off 1 st at the beginning of the next 2 rows—40 (43, 46) sts remaining. On the next RS row, begin the raglan decreases as for the back. Set the remaining 8 (9, 10) sts aside and make a second sleeve the same way, but twisting the cable to the left (C6F).

FINISHING

Leaving the live stitches on a stitch holder, iron the body and sleeves on low heat. Sew up the bottoms of the sleeves, then sew the raglan seams.

For the collar, with size 9 needles, pick up 12 (13, 14) sts on the left front (start just after the button band), then take up the live sts of the left sleeve, the back, and the right sleeve; finally, pick up 12 (13, 14) sts on the right front (stop just before the button band)—68 (75, 80) sts. Work in whimsical ribbing for 2 in./5 cm, then bind off loosely. Sew the five buttons to the right or left button band, opposite the buttonholes.

LEG WARMERS

With the size 9 needles, cast on 49 (52) sts and work in whimsical ribbing for 1.5 in./4 cm (start with 1 edge stitch, then repeat the 3-stitch rib pattern 15 (16) times, and finish with 2 knit sts and 1 edge stitch. Continue on the size 10 needles, working in stockinette stitch and cables as follows: k19 (21), p2, C6B, p2, k20 (21). On WS rows, work all the sts as they appear. When the piece measures 4.25 (4.75) in./11 (12) cm, continue in stockinette stitch all the way across, until the piece measures 7 (7.5) in./18 (19) cm. Finish with 1.5 in./4 cm of whimsical ribbing. At the same time, at 8 (8.25) in./20 (21) cm, work 12 eyelets for the pom-pom tie, distributed as follows: k2 (3), (yo, k2tog, k2) 11 (12) times, yo 1 (0) times, k2tog 1 (0) times, k1. Make the second leg warmer the same way, twisting the cable in the opposite direction (C6F).

FINISHING

Iron on low heat, then sew the side seams. With the size H-8 crochet hook, make 2 chains 140 (150) sts long. Weave these ties through the eyelets. Make 4 pompoms and attach them to the ends of the ties.

SIZES (HAT)
❉ *2/4 (6) years*

MATERIALS (HAT)
❉ *100% wool bulky weight yarn: 1 (1) hank dark gray (shown in Cascade Ecological Wool; 8.8 oz./250 g; 478 yd./437 m; Antique)*
❉ *U.S. size 9 (5.5 mm) and 10 (6 mm) straight needles*
❉ *U.S. size H-8 (5 mm) crochet hook*

HAT

With the size 9 needles, cast on 76 (82) sts and work in whimsical ribbing for 1.5 in./4 cm (start with 1 edge stitch, then work the 3-stitch rib pattern 24 (26) times, and end with 2 knit sts and 1 edge stitch). Continue on the size 10 needles, working in stockinette stitch and cables as follows: k6 (7), p2, C6B, p2, k6 (7), p2, C6F, p2, k12 (14), p2, C6B, p2, k6 (7), p2, C6F, p2, k6 (7). On WS rows, work all the sts as they appear.

When the piece measures 4.25 (4.75) in./11 (12) cm, continue in stockinette stitch. Bind off when the piece measures 7 (8) in./18 (20) cm total.

FINISHING

Iron the piece on low heat, fold in half, and sew the side and top of the hat.

Butterfly Tunic

The butterfly motif decorates the bottom edge of this tunic and gives a romantic touch that will delight little girls.

SIZES
❊ 2 (4, 6) years

MATERIALS
❊ 100% baby alpaca fine weight yarn: 3 (4, 4) hanks old rose, (shown in Blue Sky Alpacas Melange; 1.7 oz./ 50 g; 110 yd./101 m; Bubblegum)
❊ U.S. size 6 (4 mm) needles
❊ U.S. size D-3 (3.25 mm) crochet hook
❊ Yarn needle

STITCHES USED
❊ Stockinette stitch (see p. 9)
❊ Reverse stockinette stitch (see p. 9)
❊ 3-stitch picot border, using crochet slip stitch, chain, and single crochet (see p. 15)
❊ Butterfly motif

GAUGE
❊ In stockinette stitch, on size 6 needles: 20 sts x 30 rows = 4 x 4 in./10 x 10 cm.

BACK

Cast on 73 (77, 81) sts and work 4 rows of stockinette stitch. Next, work the butterfly motif to Row 14, beginning and ending each row with 0 (2, 4) sts in stockinette stitch. Continue in stockinette stitch, decreasing 1 st on each side, 1 st from the edge, when the piece measures 2 (2.25, 2.75) in./5 (6, 7) cm in all, then again at 3 (3.5, 4) in./8 (9, 10) cm, 4.25 (4.75, 5) in./11 (12, 13) cm, 5.5 (6, 6.25) in./14 (15, 16) cm, 6.5 (7, 7.5) in./17 (18, 19) cm, and finally at 8 (8.25, 8.75) in./20 (21, 22) cm. At this point you should have 61 (65, 69) sts. When the piece measures 9.5 (10.25, 11) in./24 (26, 28) cm, bind off the first 4 sts of the next 2 rows, then decrease 1 st, 1 st from the edge, at each end of every RS row, 5 times (at the beginning of the row, k1, k2tog; at the end of the row, when 3 sts remain, k2p, then k1)—43 (47, 51) sts. When the piece measures 5 (5.5, 6) in./13 (14, 15) cm from the beginning of the armhole,

bind off the 21 (23, 25) center sts and continue on the remaining 11 (12, 13) sts. Starting on the next RS row, bind off 1 st on the collar side of the piece every 2 rows, twice. Set the remaining 9 (10, 11) sts aside. Take up the 11 (12, 13) sts of the second shoulder, and work the collar decreases in mirror image, then set these 9 (10, 11) sts aside.

FRONT

Work as for the back until the piece measures 4.25 (4.75, 5) in./11 (12, 13) cm from the beginning of the sleeve hole (that is, 13.75 (15, 16) in./35 (38, 41) cm total). Work 12 (13, 14) sts, then bind off the center 19 (21, 23) sts and continue on the next 12 (13, 14) sts. Starting on the next RS row, bind off 1 st on the collar side of the piece every 2 rows, 3 times. Knit another 4 rows, then set the remaining 9 sts aside. Take up the 12 (13, 14) sts of the second shoulder and work in mirror image, then set these 9 (10, 11) sts aside.

BUTTERFLY MOTIF
Rows 1–4: Stockinette stitch.
Rows 5 and 13: *K3, p4, k5, p4, k2; repeat from * across to last st, k1.
Rows 6 and 12: *P4, k4, p3, k4, p3; repeat from * across to last st, p1.
Rows 7 and 11: *K5, p4, k1, p4, k4; repeat from * across to last st, k1.
Rows 8 and 10: *P6, k3, p1, k3, p5; repeat from * across to last st, p1.
Row 9: Knit.
Row 14: Purl.

CAP SLEEVES

Cast on 44 (50, 56) sts and work in stockinette stitch. Starting on the second row, bind off sts at the beginning of each row: 4 sts once, then 2 sts once, then 1 st once, and finally 3 sts once. Bind off the remaining 24 (30, 36) sts. Make a second cap sleeve.

FINISHING

Work the shoulder seams with the 3-needle bind-off method (see p. 15). Sew the side seams. Attach the cap sleeves just above the series of armhole decreases. Use the yarn needle to embroider antennae on the butterflies.

PICOT BORDER

With the crochet hook, work a border of picots around the collar, as follows: with the piece facing you, start on the right side. For a 3-stitch picot border, work: *2 sc, 1 sl st, ch 3, 1 sc in the same st as the sl st; repeat from * around.

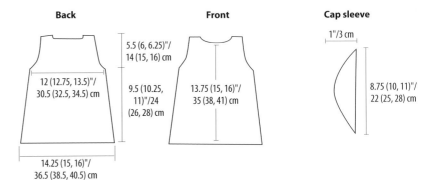

Back

5.5 (6, 6.25)"/ 14 (15, 16) cm

12 (12.75, 13.5)"/ 30.5 (32.5, 34.5) cm

9.5 (10.25, 11)"/24 (26, 28) cm

14.25 (15, 16)"/ 36.5 (38.5, 40.5) cm

Front

13.75 (15, 16)"/ 35 (38, 41) cm

Cap sleeve

1"/3 cm

8.75 (10, 11)"/ 22 (25, 28) cm